Fuel The Fire
Josiah Elias

Endorsements

Watching Josiah growing up gave me a confidence that he had a specific call upon his life. He became a student of God's Word pursuing the hidden nuggets of Scripture which resulted in a passion to deliver it. In his passion for intimacy with God, he sought after His best and became a contagious revivalist. I saw Josiah choose his bride Ashley and love her unconditionally and has become an amazing father to his daughter Emma Faith and his son Judah David. He is well balanced in his approach to family and ministry and I'm proud to say he is one who leads well and will impact many for God's glory.

George Elias
Proud father
Author: Jesus of Nazareth, Faithful and Free

Josiah is passionate about pleasing God, being led by the Spirit, and leading people in a practical and understandable way. I have watched his hands-on approach to personally disciple individuals seeing them grow into fully devoted followers of Christ and productive church attenders. He has a unique way of bringing out the best in those around him and helping them to discover untapped gifts they didn't know they had. It's an honor to watch a young man operate in his calling while keeping his priorities securely in place. He's a world changer and I know your life will be impacted by his ministry.

Brian Ross
Lead Pastor - Faith Chapel San Diego
www.faithchapelsd.com

Tenacious, determined and driven, with a magnetic personality that drew people to him and now to his precious and loving LORD. This is how I knew Josiah as I watched him grow into the man of God he is today. In this work of anointed art, "Fuel The Fire", you will see his personality as he draws you to Christ and His love for you. If you find yourself lacking in your first love for Christ, you will discover yourself desiring to return to God's burning love. "Fuel The Fire" is that powerfully anointed! Written in the simplest manner, the book unfolds God, as the source of all a man or a woman needs to be whole. You will see again, Jesus Christ, in His ministry to you and His redeeming grace. You will see the Holy Spirit at work for your benefit to see your life change as He teaches you to remove all religious limitations.

Those of you who read this writing with careful thought and diligence will find yourselves forgiven, forgiving, renewed, encouraged and more thoroughly grounded in your faith to change the world around you. Enjoy, and Shalom.

Cesar Ochoa (Tio)
Mentor - Uncle to Josiah Elias

I have known Josiah for the better part of ten years. I've watched him grow from a zealous youth to a passionate preacher, a courageous pastor, to a loving father and devoted husband. His language and faith are shared and clearly communicated through all he does. I'm grateful for the time I get with he and his family as I enjoy a front row seat and watch their story unfold. I consider it an honor and a privilege to know them and I believe Josiah is just getting started, a spirit of revival follows him everywhere he goes.

Jake Hamilton
Author, singer, song-writer
www.jakehamiltonmusic.com

Contents

Acknowledgements

Special thanks to Amy Mundo for her incredible editing talents and treasured encouragements to me through this journey. You made this journey a joy for me and kept me excited to keep moving forward. I also want to say thank you for inviting Ashley to that conference in 2009 where God introduced me to her.
The rest is history and I am forever grateful.

Special thanks to Tim Maxwell for his artistic skills and willingness to serve the King in any opportunity that presents itself. Your support and friendship is such a blessing to me. Thank you for loving God like you do. Tim.claygraphics@gmail.com

Finally, thank you to my beautiful family. To my precious kids who would not fall asleep without mommy and daddy present. It was while I put you to sleep each night that I wrote this book. Watching you sleep was a powerful motivation for me to keep writing in hopes that I could impact moms and dads to burn for God for the sake of their families. My passion for God is my greatest gift to you. To my gorgeous bride who supported me through this wild journey, thank you for believing in me. Thank you for praying tirelessly for me and for choosing to love me every day. You mean more to me than any other person on the planet. I love you Ashley.

INTRODUCTION

"I'm on fire for God!" Have you ever heard that expression or said it yourself? Most of us probably have. When we say this, I believe we're trying to communicate that God is absolutely rocking our world. We're hungry, passionate, zealous, excited, overwhelmed, grateful, at peace, about to lose our minds, wildly in love with Jesus! I hope this is your present reality. I've had times in my life where this was exactly how I felt, and times when these several descriptive words weren't describing me at all. I wouldn't say that I ever stopped loving God, but my flame surely dwindled. Sin crept in and kicked dirt on the fire burning deep within me, smothering it. I got lazy. I became self-absorbed. My priorities were focused elsewhere. Friends took center stage. Money became all too important. Relationships ate up my time and energy. More dirt. Before I knew it, my once raging inferno was a flickering flame. I needed fuel for the fire. I needed to rid myself of all the things that were choking out the oxygen so the flame could breathe and grow. I needed to repent. I needed to change the way I thought. I needed to reprioritize. I needed to destroy some things while building some other things. I had to purge unhealthy relationships from my life while establishing God-centered new ones. I needed to spend my time better.

Obviously, there were several adjustments that needed to be made in my life, and I would probably guess that if you asked the Holy Spirit to help show you some things in your life that needed to be adjusted, He might have a suggestion or two. This never ends. Our Christian walk is not a straight line. We're constantly course correcting our path. We're making adjustments as we let the Spirit lead us one day at a time.

My heart, which I believe to be aligned with God's heart for this book, is to fuel the fire for God that is burning deep within you. I want to share with you some tools I've discovered that have fueled my passion for the King and His Kingdom. I also want to provoke you to be bold enough to identify the things that are smothering your flame and put courage into you to get rid of them. My prayer is that Almighty God would draw so near to you as you draw near to Him through these pages. I know He will highlight things we'll cover and burn them deep into you. If you're willing to read with the intent of not being entertained but rather to fall more in love with God than you currently are, I have no doubt you'll succeed.

Precious King, I welcome You into this journey. Help me to fall deeper in love with You than ever before. Fuel the fire You sparked in me when I gave my heart to You. Stash kindling in my spirit, soul, and body so that everything that makes me, me would burn intensely. I want to burn bright for all to see, long to stand the test of time, loud for all to hear, and hot for all to feel. Make me contagious and courageous. I give You permission to do as You see fit in my life. Reveal the things that need to change and change the things that You reveal as I submit to Your will. I love You, precious Holy Spirit. I love You, King Jesus. I love You, Father with all that is within me. Amen.

If you've never given your heart to Jesus and made Him both Lord and Savior of your life, or your heart has grown cold towards God, there is no time like right now. He loves you, far more than I could ever explain. When He went to the cross two-thousand years ago, He was thinking of you. He couldn't stand to spend eternity in Heaven without you. All you have to do, is give Him everything. That's right, just everything you have and all that you are! I won't sugarcoat it for you, the Gospel is simple, but it'll cost you

7

everything. Here's the best part, when you and I give Him our messed up, broken, hurting, dysfunctional lives, He takes our broken pieces and builds a masterpiece. He calls us sons and daughters. He destroys our sins and remembers them no more. His blood, that He shed on the cross, completely wipes it away. He welcomes you and I into His Kingdom which is moving and active here on the earth and will be forever in Heaven, the place all who make this decision go to when they die. It's a pretty sweet deal.

It doesn't really matter what words you choose when you ask Jesus to come be Lord of your life, but what really matters is that they come from your heart with complete sincerity. It's not the prayer that saves you; it's the faith attached to what you pray that makes all the difference. Tell Him how you feel. Be honest. He's a big boy; He can handle your honesty. Ask Him to be both Lord and Savior. If He's just Savior, you'll make it to Heaven when you die but you'll never experience Heaven on earth. If He's your Lord, your Master, your Guide, then you'll have Heaven on earth as well as for the rest of eternity. He'll teach you how to live a life that pleases Him. This prayer is not a "get out of hell free card." It's an opportunity to begin a relationship with God.

He's real and He's been waiting for you. Romancing you. Drawing you close to Him because His love for you is relentless. He's been orchestrating some phenomenal things behind the scenes to get this message to you because He's that detailed and cares for you that much. He wants to heal you. Provide for you. Restore you. Strengthen you. Correct you. Applaud you. Save you. You are one honest prayer away from beginning this journey. It's a journey that will last a lifetime. Pray that prayer in your own words and allow me to help fuel the new fire burning within you. You can do this. Let's burn together.

8

1

PROTOTYPE

Jesus is the prototype of what a human in right relationship with God can do. Something happens when we read the Scriptures and study the life of Jesus in order to discover what possibilities are available to us. If Jesus came to the earth only as God, it's still amazing. But He didn't come just as God, He also came as man. Now, His coming and all He's done is absolutely amazing but it is also provoking. Throughout His ministry, He constantly modeled to His disciples what a Kingdom mindset looks like on a day-to-day basis.

When Jesus fed the five thousand families with just five loaves and two fish, He was modeling to His followers that they didn't ever have to worry about a food problem. He could handle it. Unfortunately, they didn't learn the lesson. They didn't see Jesus as the prototype for what they could do in the future. The next time there was a major food problem, they clearly hadn't changed the way they thought. Now, four thousand families are hungry and Jesus has seven loaves of bread and a few small fish. He's going to give the lesson to them again. He's once again modeling that a food issue is no issue at all if you can believe that He is the Provider. Sure enough, He feeds the four thousand just like before. It apparently didn't matter how many loaves of bread or fishes He had to begin with. He could feed as many as were hungry with whatever was available. I tend to believe that even if He had no bread or fish to start with, He could still feed as many as were hungry.

While Israel wandered in the wilderness, water poured forth from a rock so multitudes could drink. He can do it all and this is worth celebrating! However, don't stop there. Learn the lesson that took the disciples at least two times to get. Don't just believe that He can do it, believe that we can do it too. This is the shifting of the mind He wants for each one of us. Throughout the rest of the Bible we don't see another food shortage problem among the apostles. Apparently they got it.

There is a fine line between pride and understanding identity. If you understand that you are a son or daughter of the King, you'll know that you are awesome and you have access to everything the King says you can have access too. That's not pride, unless you let it become pride. The reality is, you are awesome! But you're only awesome because He has made you awesome. Still, that makes you awesome. Did you catch that? Sometimes it appears that people are so scared to fall into pride that they reflect any compliment or any good thing they do immediately to the Lord in some fashion of false humility and never stop to simply say, "Thank You! Praise God." The motive may be good but the end result is not best. What I'm getting at is this, don't wait around forever hoping God will come and do something in your midst because He is awesome. He's already made you incredible and He's put His Spirit within you. Start getting your hands dirty now and watch the favor of God unfold as you move forward. Jesus as our prototype would have failed miserably if duplicates were never made. A prototype by definition is the original model, and Jesus was a perfect original model. He may be the original, but as Christians we have all the same ingredients He had. He designed it this way. That makes us kind of a big deal. Again, not pride, just true identity.

Jesus got incredible glory for His Father when He walked the earth and moved in the supernatural. God gets even more glory when we, His sons and daughters step up and do the same. Our frail, human, imperfect, yet believing selves doing the things that He says we can do brings Him great glory! People need to see the power of God through you. Your life is the canvas that God wants to use to paint the picture of His Son, the King of the Kingdom. This goes for every person out there. People from every nationality, every social economic status, every personality type. Each individual is a unique brush-stroke of a unique color upon a grand painting.

Jesus didn't do anything that He didn't first see the Father do. So where were His eyes fixated? On the Father. If He's the prototype…the permission granting life for each one of us, where should our eyes be fixated? On the Father. Now, you may be thinking that you don't know what the Father is saying or doing. It's simple, look at Jesus. He said, **"…Anyone who has seen Me has seen the Father!…"** **(John 14:9 NLT)** Jesus perfectly revealed to us the Father. So fix our eyes on Him. Train your brain to read about Jesus in the Scriptures and to listen to what He's actively doing in the earth today and let that inspire you to begin walking in the very same thing.

The day my wife, Ashley, left her relationship with her boyfriend for God, she walked away feeling relieved and troubled all in the same moment. She knew she was being obedient to God and was taking a stand for her faith in perhaps the most pivotal moment of her life, but she was also venturing into a whole new world. When she walked out of the building she wondered, "What am I going to eat?" She relied on him for everything, even her meals. She didn't have a lot of money and even something as normal as eating was about to become a challenge. Right after she had this thought, a random person at the building she was at asked out loud, "Does anybody want a chicken?" She immediately started crying. She knew that it was now God's job to provide for her and apparently He was already busy at doing so. She didn't have to rely on an unhealthy relationship anymore, she could rely solely on Him. She not only got a chicken to eat but also a huge tray of beef ribs. The timing of the Lord was incredible.

He was teaching her in that moment that if she would be obedient to Him and remain faithful to her love for Him, He would take care of her. To this day, she has never gone hungry. She has shifted the way that she thinks. That's the key. The goal was never just to get her a chicken or a single meal. The goal of the Father was to teach her to change the way she thinks. If the Father would care for His Son flawlessly, she could rest assured knowing He would care for her flawlessly.

This very idea of Jesus being the prototype for what's available to us challenges our pseudo-comfort. Things are a lot easier when we can just remain where we're at and never dig out our potential. I, for one, am not looking for easier. I am looking at Jesus and He certainly didn't take the easy road on anything. It was never about easy, it was always about obedience to what He saw His Father doing. The Father has always been pulling the best out of each of us.

When I look at my kids, I don't want to give them the easiest life I can give them, I want to set the stage for the most passionately devoted-to-God lifestyle I possibly can. Much of the time, that is not easy. In many ways it's not comfortable. However, don't forget, His name is Comforter. So much of what we label comfort is actually a pseudo-comfort. Nearness to Him and obedience to His voice births a comfort that can't be found in anything else. The mirage of comfort is paralyzing much of the church. If the Holy Spirit is leading you into the most tumultuous of situations, but it's where He is, then that situation is the most comfortable place you could be. It is where He is. Look at our prototype; He is sleeping through storms. Crowds are gathering to stone Him and He manages to quietly slip through the crowd. He's about to be crucified and He advances to a quiet garden at night to be with His Father. Sweating blood, yet comfortable. We need a paradigm shift concerning our understanding of comfort. Jesus changed it all.

"All praise to God, the Father of our Lord Jesus Christ. God is our merciful Father and the source of all comfort. He comforts us in all our troubles so that we can comfort others. When they are troubled, we will be able to give them the same comfort God has given us. For the more we suffer for Christ, the more God will shower us with his comfort through Christ. Even when we are weighed down with troubles, it is for your comfort and salvation! For when we ourselves are comforted, we will certainly comfort you. Then you can patiently endure the same things we suffer. We are confident that as you share in our sufferings, you will also share in the comfort God gives us." (2 Cor. 1:3-7 NLT)

You can see the life of Jesus one of two ways. Amazing and that's it. Or, amazing so mine can be amazing too. I know what Jesus would prefer for you. That's why He is our prototype for Kingdom living. Step into your destiny. It's not so much about what you'll do…it's far more about who you are meant to be.

2
THE ONE LAMB

I have often wondered what makes God sovereignly select certain people to do extraordinary things. Abraham to birth a nation. Moses to deliver a people. Mary to carry the Son of God within her womb. There are several indicators in each story as to why they were selected for the job and it's fascinating to dissect each of them. Before David was king, he was a shepherd boy worshipping God amongst his father's sheep. We receive several clues that play into why God selected somebody like David for such a remarkable destiny. Perhaps his heart of worship. His humility. His faith. These are all contributors, but I want to focus on one particular characteristic of David we all so desperately need.

Let me paint a little picture for you. David is anointed king by the prophet Samuel instead of his father Jesse's choice son Eliab, who by appearances alone would best be suited for kingship. But the Lord doesn't measure a man by his physical appearance, rather the Lord looks at the heart. So after confirming none of Jesse's choice sons to be king, the prophet Samuel asks if there is anyone else. Jesse resorts to David, still out tending the sheep. Clearly, he was not valued enough by his father Jesse to even be invited to come inside when the prophet was visiting their home. After finally being invited in, the Lord tells Samuel that this is the one He has chosen.

David is anointed king by Samuel but is not instituted as king just yet. In the eyes of Heaven, David will be king, but in the eyes of the world this has yet to actually happen. Now, shortly after this, the army of Israel and the army of the Philistines are encamped against each other. There is a valley between them and each day for forty days, a giant named Goliath, an intense warrior, has come out and taunted the armies of Israel, challenging them to a fight, to which nobody has responded. The challenge is to put the Philistines champion, Goliath, against whomever is Israel's champion and let the two of them duke it out with the loser's army becoming slaves to the winner's. David shows up, bringing some food to his older brothers and hears what's going on:

> Then David said to Saul, "Let no man's heart fail because of him; your servant will go and fight with this Philistine."
> And Saul said to David, "You are not able to go against this Philistine to fight with him; for you are a youth, and he a man of war from his youth."
> But David said to Saul, "Your servant used to keep his father's sheep, and when a lion or a bear came and took a lamb out of the flock, I went out after it and struck it, and delivered the lamb from its mouth; and when it arose against me, I caught it by its beard, and struck and killed it. (1 Sam. 17:32-35 NKJV)

Hold up! "When a lion or bear came and took <u>a lamb</u> out of the flock…" Now David, it doesn't even seem very reasonable for you to risk your life to go retrieve just one lamb that the lion or bear is snatching from the flock. If they're invading the whole flock and killing all your sheep then sure, go put an end to it but we are just talking about one lamb. It's not that big of a deal. Admittedly, this is the mindset I would have if I were in David's shoes…or sandals. I could spare a lamb or two here and there if it means I keep my life. Especially if I know that I'm going to be king sometime in the near future. Better not risk my life on something so petty; I have got bigger things to attend to.

But apparently, David's character was far greater than my own, and he refused to allow even one lamb under his watch to be taken from him. I believe this beautiful quality of David is one of the contributing factors that positioned him to be chosen by God to be king of Israel. This quality David possessed was integrity.

David's integrity would not allow even a crack to come upon the wall of protection he built for his sheep. Each one was important to him. Most people tend to think big picture and would only risk their lives confronting a lion or bear if, in their minds, they could justify the risk. Most people's integrity would not measure up to David's. But I believe David understood something most of us do not, it is the small cracks in our foundation that compromise the whole.

I believe the devil knows he cannot just send lions and bears storming into our lives, wreaking havoc. If he did, we would surely not tolerate the attacks and we would stand up to him. But if the devil can offer us spoonfuls of compromise, one lamb at a time, we will allow the cracks on our character to grow slowly but surely until our entire foundation is destroyed.

The devil typically does not come into my life tempting me to start experimenting with hard drugs, mass genocide and gun running…nope, he introduces spoonfuls of compromise by tempting me to justify my not praying because I have had a long day. Temptations come in the form of not reading the Word of God consistently, comparing myself to other leaders around me, glancing twice at a beautiful woman, trying to take the problems of life head-on under my own power instead of trusting Him. When we give in to allowing the devil, *who walks around like a roaring lion seeking whom he may devour (1 Pet. 5:8)* the satisfaction of having just one lamb, we empower him to help himself to another. Then another, and another until before we know it, we find ourselves in a deep, dark pit and wonder how we got there in the first place. That lack of integrity with the one lamb is what spirals us out of control and often lands us in a place we never thought we would be. But it all begins with those spoonfuls of compromise.

David was confident to face Goliath because he had his integrity intact. '"**Your servant has killed both lion and bear; and this uncircumcised Philistine will be like one of them, seeing he has defied the armies of the living God.'**

Moreover David said, 'The LORD, who delivered me from the paw of the lion and from the paw of the bear, He will deliver me from the hand of this Philistine'" (1 Sam. 17:36-37 NKJV).

David just got done saying that he was the one who killed the lion and the bear by taking it by its beard, striking it, and killing it, but then he says that it was the Lord who delivered him. David's humility accompanying his integrity has positioned him favorably in the sight of the Lord. It is becoming clearer and clearer to see why David was a man after God's own heart (Acts 13:22). Even though he was the one who took care of the lion and the bear—his strength, courage, boldness, and confidence came from the Lord. No wonder he was so confident to face Goliath.

David was ready for Goliath because he knew who his God was, and he knew his integrity was intact. Lack of integrity will always hinder our walk with the Lord. On the other hand, maintained integrity will always fortify our walk with the Lord. David was full of confidence, ready to stand against giants cursing his God, his nation, his king, and his family. Wow! Do you realize that within hours of David even hearing about Goliath, he had killed him? Goliath had been single-handedly taunting an entire army for 40 days, and nobody had done anything about it until David, who within hours, had cut off his head!

I believe that the attempts to rob David of the one lamb in the fields was in hopes to crack his integrity so that one day he would not be ready for the giant.

I recently had a dream dealing with integrity and growing a backbone. In the dream, there was an individual who I'd had conflict with in the past now attempting to come back to our ministry. I wanted reconciliation, but I could tell that there was no change in this person's character or behavior. I was torn. I wanted us to be cool again, but I did not want to compromise intolerance for his behavior.

The dream scene shifts, and I find myself in a store with a few of my CORE Leaders. They began stealing some minor things from the store like candy and hair gel but stealing nonetheless. Then another one of them stole a couple dirty magazines from behind the counter. They put all these things in their bags and walked out. I once again was tempted to ignore what they had just done. After all, these were my friends, and we were hanging out together for the day, I didn't want things to get awkward.

Shortly after leaving the store, the owner came rushing out, demanding to get back the items they had just stolen. I finally grew a backbone in that moment and reprimanded my friends. "No! You can't do this! What's wrong with you?" I shouted, knowing this would hinder our friendship. I took the bags away from them and took away the stolen items except for the dirty magazines. Even though I was standing up to them, I still felt tempted to compromise in allowing those to remain. Then suddenly the dream ended.

This dream is laced with lessons on character and integrity. I knew that by standing up to my friends I was going to hinder my relationship with them, but I didn't care. I wanted to do the right thing. Even while I was correcting them I was still tempted to let them get away with a little. Perhaps so they would feel that it was not a total loss. I was people pleasing.

These little bits of compromise crack our character and ensure we are not ready when it's our turn to face the giants. I knew from this dream that God was encouraging me to live uncompromisingly and to grow a backbone when it comes to the areas of my life that I tolerate the behavior of others around me. Just because they're my friends, or they're from my church does not make it ok for them to act a certain way. If I allow that behavior in my presence, then I essentially condone it. If I condone it, then I might as well be doing it myself. We in the church cannot allow the one lamb to be stolen from right under our noses.

In 2004, NASA's Genesis space capsule crashed in the Utah desert because a critical piece of equipment was installed backwards. Millions of dollars and years of time and data were lost due to a seemingly minor detail. This was indeed a major dilemma. Ask yourself what lambs are being robbed from you on a continual basis? What sort of things are seemingly not a big deal to give up but perhaps God is revealing to you that the enemy's bears and lions are busy at work against you? Remember, they may be subtle or minor. But in the grand scheme of things, those minor cracks in crucial areas of our lives become major quite quickly. Don't compromise surrendering even one lamb.

3
INCONVENIENT CHRISTIANITY

The nature of true Christianity is sacrifice. Sacrifice necessitates inconvenience. Oh, I already know that most Christians hate this, especially in America. We are only a few sentences into this chapter and you may already be feeling uncomfortable with these opening statements. Or, perhaps you feel challenged. This is foremost my prayer for you. However, the truth is, by and large, that we have become spoiled and babied. Most of the American church wants their fast food Jesus as convenient as possible. The very thought of inconvenient Christianity puts a bad taste in our mouths. Having known really nothing other than the American church, I have fallen victim to, spectator of, and now combatant against this casual Christianity.

Convenient Christianity has taught us that the shorter the service, the better. The less that is demanded of us, the happier we will be. The more you rub our backs, scratch our itches, and tickle our emotions the better chances you will have of us coming back next week. The over-the-top entertaining service is all that keeps our attention. We don't see value in communication with God unless it's a prayer before a meal or we find ourselves in dire need. The extent of us actually reading the Word of God comes in the form of liking or sharing a verse somebody else posts on social media. Our idea of worship looks less and less Biblical yet more and more self-serving. There is little to no sacrifice and which means little to no inconvenience.

Somehow, I doubt this is what Jesus had in mind when He poured out His Spirit on the early church. The "greater things we will do" promise doesn't seem to fit what I am currently seeing all around the nation. When I read the pages of the precious Word of God and then take a look around at what so many are calling "successful ministries" and "on-fire Christians," I discover a massive disconnect. I believe that the Father designed those following Jesus to truly be inconvenienced because He knew that narrow would be the way and few there are that would find it. Finding Him is intentionally inconvenient. He knew the steep price that both He, the Father and His Son, Jesus, would have to pay in order to redeem humanity. He saw how dishonoring it would be to make salvation so cheap. Make no mistake about it, salvation is free, but it costs you everything! It's so expensive, so pricy, so valuable that nobody could pay for it, so it had to be free for anybody to have it. Nobody casually strolls into salvation. It's a passionate decision of the heart. It's an inconvenient step of faith into the greatest blessing anyone could ever receive. It's the receptivity and participation of the greatest transaction in the history of humanity.

Whenever I give an altar call, I flirt with the idea of making it as inconvenient as possible. Sometimes I do, sometimes I don't, depending on the moment and the audience. What I refuse to do is try to get as many hands raised as possible, knowing that I'm not giving true salvation any justice in my proposal of what it really costs. This thought first struck me very early on in ministry. Week after week hands would go up in response to salvation calls. I would joyfully tell friends and family the numbers of those being saved. As time went on, I began to wonder where all these people who were being saved were at. They sure weren't in my ministry because we weren't really growing that fast. I would often cast out a safety net response that they were probably getting plugged into other ministries in the area, but which ones? I developed relationships with other ministries within the area and rarely if ever saw those who had supposedly given their lives to Jesus there either.

The truth hit me pretty hard. It's more than likely that these individuals weren't really getting saved. They were probably having a beautiful emotional experience in the moment and perhaps really wanting to become a follower of Christ but for my lack of appropriate proposal of what Christianity truly is or the all to convenient system of response, they were not truly changing. This strikes fear in my heart. What if some thought that if they just raised their hand at the salvation call, BOOM, they'd go to Heaven? That's on me. Ministers walk a fine line between wanting visitors in particular to feel comfortable in our churches and the nature of the Gospel itself that challenges our comfort. My heart is not to keep people from responding by raising their hands, rather it's to better and more vividly portray what raising their hands in that moment actually means.

Sometimes I feel it's all too easy and convenient for someone to sheepishly raise their hand half-way up while everybody's heads are bowed and eyes are closed. I fully understand why we so often do this in the church, but I also think that the convenience of this response to the sacred call of God into His Kingdom is potentially backfiring. I believe that our American churches are filling with people who think that because they half-raised their hand in the back of a crowd at the end of a Sunday sermon sometime in the past they are now saved and wholly transformed. Done. Check that off the list.

Now, I believe that a decision made in faith to choose Jesus Christ as both Lord and Savior literally happens in a single moment. Otherwise the thief on the cross that Jesus told would be with Him in Paradise that day was lied to. Something happened in that specific moment. I recently was asked to come minister to an older man dying of cancer. In our short conversation, I was able to lead him to the Lord where He made a confession of faith in Jesus Christ. It was beautiful! He died only a few days later. The family is certainly mourning the loss but there is a wonderful comfort knowing where he will spend eternity. However, for the most part, the vast majority of people that choose to follow Jesus are not on their death beds. They'll have to truly weigh out their decision to become a Christian and factor in what that means for the rest of their lives.

It is the responsibility of those who are already Christians to adequately explain this to those making the decision. In many ways, we've failed at this. Consequently, our churches are filled with thousands upon thousands of false conversions. These people don't realize that the prayer of repentance at the altar is not where everything finishes but where everything begins. Praying the sinner's prayer is the first step of a wonderfully glorious and inconvenient journey both into the Father's arms day by day and by walking with the Father hand in hand through life. We're constantly changing through the consecrating work of the Spirit making us look and live more like Jesus. While at the same time lunging into the destiny Almighty God dreamt up for us long before we were brought into this world.

This journey we're on, is an inconvenient journey. Jesus told His disciples when He was sending them out to minister on their own for the first time:

> **Don't take any money in your money belts—no gold, silver, or even copper coins. Don't carry a traveler's bag with a change of clothes and sandals or even a walking stick...Look, I am sending you out as sheep among wolves. So be as shrewd as snakes and harmless as doves. But beware! For you will be handed over to the courts and will be flogged with whips in the synagogues. You will stand trial before**

governors and kings because you are my followers... (Matt. 10:9-10; 16-18 NLT)

It appears that Jesus is deliberately making this as inconvenient as possible. The greater the inconvenience, the greater the opportunity for faith to manifest. Jesus knew this. It was part of His plan all along. He is always attempting to pull faith out of us. Through our journey of inconvenience, we naturally stimulate faith, which is pleasing to God, for without faith it is impossible to please Him.

I highly value discipleship. Jesus modeled discipleship, and I don't think we should do any less. When somebody wants me to disciple them, if I'm able, I almost always joyfully say yes. For the first couple meetings, I get to know the individual, and I make sure they fully understand what they're getting themselves into. I pursue them constantly during this period. Then after a few weeks of this, I stop calling them. I don't remind them of our next meeting. I don't follow up with how they're doing on their homework or much of anything else. When I see them I'm still very friendly with them and love on them, but I don't make the push that I do at the beginning. I'm curious if they're still going to pursue being discipled even if it becomes increasingly inconvenient for them. I want to see how much they value it. Are they just going to come simply because I am pushing them too? Or are they determined to grow no matter the adversity.

I know a day will come when I won't be able to be there for them for whatever reason, and I don't want their successes in the Lord to be based upon my aggressive involvement. The truly hungry ones follow up with me. They contact me and make sure that everything is good and our meeting is still on. Almost everybody is momentarily taken back when they realize that my reaching out to them suddenly stopped. The ones who are concerned about this stand out to me. Clearly, they are taking this seriously and their response proves they don't want our meetings to stop or their growth to cease. I am convinced that nothing can keep you from growing in the Lord if you are determined to do so. Nothing.

On the flip side, there are many that seem to lose interest in discipleship the moment I stop pursuing them. Basically communicating that my absence became their way out. The discipleship meeting was never for my gain to begin with anyways, it was for their growth. If they don't really want to do it or perhaps they are not ready, that's fine. But pouring into a vessel with holes seems unproductive for both us.

Many people start off with the right motives and are full of excitement to get discipled, but once they realize what's demanded of a healthy growing Christian, they fold. The inconvenience slaughters them. This is so unfortunate, yet fine with me. It is not that they are a bad person or that they don't love God. It's just that they are not ready, which is okay. Well, it's not okay considering the scope of eternity, but I mean to say that I understand why some people just aren't ready to lay it all down. Still, I'm not going to spend precious time on those who are not willing to inconvenience themselves to grow in the things of God, becoming a disciple which Jesus commanded each of us both to become and to make. This somewhat risky method has probably saved me hundreds of hours of seed sowing onto unready soil. But when a person is good soil, ready to take on the challenges that lay ahead of them and willing do what it takes to draw nearer to the One Who promises to draw near to them if they'll take the necessary steps, it's always an honor to pour into them.

I don't know where we get off thinking that He owes us something. Like our coming to church is somehow doing God a favor. This sense of entitlement is destroying the American church from within. Insecure pastors now bend over backwards to try to get you to come back next week. Since these pastors are supposedly men of God, entitled individuals think that by showing up at an event they are doing that man of God a favor, thus doing God a favor. Let me be ridiculously clear…God does not need you! He wants you. You and I get to participate in becoming the Bride of Christ, but even if we choose not to, Jesus will still get His Bride! Whether we choose to be a part of Her or not. God will be just fine without you, but it breaks His heart when we are far from Him. He does not need our service, but He loves to partner with His children for His purposes in the earth. He does not need our tithe…but our giving releases His blessings into our lives and advances His Kingdom.

God does not fall off the throne when we don't come to church, whatever our excuse is. However, we might need to check our hearts if we find ourselves not wanting to be at church or becoming flaky with our commitments. Why don't we want to be in the house of God where His sons and daughters gather to worship and grow together? Is a weekly diet of church attendance too inconvenient within our crazy schedules?

I believe the closer we get to God, the more we fall in love with His Bride, the Church. For those who claim to love God but hate the Church, I would say there is something wrong with them. You cannot claim to love the Bridegroom but hate His Bride. If somebody told me they loved me but couldn't stand my wife—those would be fighting words. Fall deeper in love with Jesus, and you'll fall deeper in love with His church and all she's destined to do in the earth.

We cannot claim that Yahweh is God, and give him an hour and a half a week when we give our jobs 40+ hours a week. Where we spend our time, our money, our efforts, and our attention is likely where our God is. Take a moment and reflect on what you claim to value. If God is at the top of the list, as He should be, how much time, money, efforts, and attention is He getting from you?

He certainly is a jealous God. His name is Jehovah Kanna- The Lord Who is Jealous. He is not a jealous girlfriend acting all crazy, following you around and throwing a fit over every little thing you do, but He is so passionately in love with you that it breaks His heart to watch those who claim to love Him in bed with other lovers. We prostitute ourselves to the gods of this world chasing our time, money, efforts, and attention while Yahweh Himself is beckoning us to allow His jealous love to overcome us.

Often what we have placed before the Lord is not a bad thing it's just not the best thing. For example, our families. I have a beautiful bride of almost eight years right now and two small children. Emma, who is currently almost four and Judah, who is two. I love my family! I spend lots of time, money, effort, and attention on my family but not more than I spend on my God. He is my first love. Somehow by putting God even before my wife, I'm enabled to love her even greater because my love for Him is foremost. Almost like an upside-down funnel—I stay connected to the one thing that matters, and my capacity to love on the other end is enlarged. I've discovered how to bring the love and passion for my God into my family. We worship together, pray together, sing together, dance together, discuss God together. He is at the center of my family.

What other good things do you spend your time, money, effort, and attention on? Your career? Your hobbies? Your friends? Consider bringing God into those good things. This keeps Him as top priority and keeps us from prostituting ourselves to the highest bidder.

In Matthew 15, there is a fascinating story of a woman who would stop at nothing to get a breakthrough for her demonized daughter.

"Then Jesus left Galilee and went north to the region of Tyre and Sidon" (Matt. 15:21 NLT).

First, notice that Jesus is in Gentile territory, not Jewish territory.

> **A Gentile woman who lived there came to him, pleading, "Have mercy on me, O Lord, Son of David! For my daughter is possessed by a demon that torments her severely.**
> **But Jesus gave her no reply, not even a word. Then his disciples urged him to send her away. "Tell her to go away," they said. "She is bothering us with all her begging." (Matt. 15:22-23 NLT)**

Ouch Jesus, that's a little harsh. Apparently the disciples just don't quite get it yet.

> **Then Jesus said to the woman, "I was sent only to help God's lost sheep—the people of Israel."**
> **But she came and worshiped him, pleading again, "Lord, help me!"**
> **Jesus responded, "It isn't right to take food from the children and throw it to the dogs." (Matt. 15:24-26 NLT)**

Whoa! Okay now, it was bad enough that You were ignoring her, but do You have to go and insult the lady? That doesn't sound very Jesus-like.

"She replied, 'That's true, Lord, but even dogs are allowed to eat the scraps that fall beneath their masters' table'" (Matt. 15:27 NLT).

I like this lady. Her response rocks me. I may be a dog, but at least I'm at the right table.

"'Dear woman,' Jesus said to her, 'your faith is great. Your request is granted.' And her daughter was instantly healed'" (Matt. 15:28 NLT).

Jesus is seemingly stiff-arming this lady in the face, but hidden within His "insult" was an invitation. He was actually attempting to draw her in. He was seeing how desperate she truly was. Was she going to give up because Jesus kept walking and apparently was not going to give her the time of day? Was she going to throw in the towel on her daughter's deliverance because the disciples of Jesus were trying to get her to leave Jesus alone? Apparently not. She continued to worship Him and cried out for help. When she finally got the attention of Jesus, I think Jesus was more excited than she was. But His acting skills were on point, so He pushed back at her one more time with an insult to see if she was still willing to go one step further and of course she was. She knew His goodness and placed a demand on it, recognizing that she was not much in the eyes of anybody—but even a nobody full of faith can become a somebody to Jesus and gain the attention of the Son of God, and miracles can happen.

Jesus did not make this easy for her. Jesus did not make it convenient for her to get her miracle. Everything she was doing was noble. She was not even pressing in for her own personal miracle, but for that of her daughter! This is the exact type of person that Jesus should be looking to touch, right? Still, He does not make it convenient for her. Why? I believe that Jesus was teaching in this very moment. Not just this woman and whomever else was watching, but knowing this would be recorded for billions to eaves drop in on for centuries to come. Are we willing to push like this woman had to? Are we hungry enough that even when it appears that Jesus Himself doesn't want you there, that He may be mad at you, you can bank on His goodness and continue to cry out, full of faith, knowing that He hears you?

We give up all too easily. I wonder how many miracles I have aborted because I stopped too short. I have felt led of the Spirit to pray for somebody with an obvious physical ailment, and so I pray, for about two minutes…then when nothing happens I dish out a "God bless you…" and be on my way. I wonder how many circumstances I have been in where God was indeed wanting to demonstrate His power, but unlike this lady in Matthew 15, I backed away. I didn't have eyes to see He was actually drawing me in. Perhaps I didn't recognize that within His apparent stiff-arm was actually a beckoning. I don't want to make those mistakes any longer, and I pray you don't either. It is certainly inconvenient to give those extra several minutes. It is certainly inconvenient to step out in faith, perhaps at the grocery store or workplace, believing for the power of the Spirit to be demonstrated. And that's exactly how He likes it. Are you desperate for breakthrough, yet? Hungry enough to keep knocking, crying, praying, believing when it appears that nobody else is?

A similar and powerful story is told right after the account we just read:

> **Jesus returned to the Sea of Galilee and climbed a hill and sat down.**
> **A vast crowd brought to him people who were lame, blind, crippled, those who couldn't speak, and many others. They laid them before Jesus, and he healed them all.**

The crowd was amazed! Those who hadn't been able to speak were talking, the crippled were made well, the lame were walking, and the blind could see again! And they praised the God of Israel. (Matt. 15:29-31 NLT)

Did you catch that before Jesus started ministering to these sick people, He first climbed a hill? Jesus, don't You think that it would be far more convenient to heal these lame, crippled, and blind people on level ground or perhaps at a local Starbucks where there is AC and vanilla lattes? Jesus would most likely reply, "Yep, it probably would be far more convenient." Then He would climb up the hill anyway.

Jesus knew that those who were desperate enough to get up the hill to where He was seated, would get what they came for. They had to first demonstrate their faith to climb the mountain to get to Him before they could petition for a miracle. They had to let their hunger for breakthrough override their desire for convenience.

I wonder how many people Jesus saw starting up that hillside that put a smile on His face. I am sure He was praying for them atop the mountain, for the angels of God to encourage them, to strengthen them to keep going. Not to give up. There may have been a person there that day without legs, but if he was willing to crawl his way up that mountain, he would surely be sprinting back down after his encounter with Jesus. I am also curious how many people heard that Jesus was in town, saw Him way up on the hillside and because of their physical dysfunction said, "Never mind." Their lack of faith and unwillingness to be inconvenienced cost them their breakthrough.

In Luke chapter 19, a tax collector named Zacchaeus encounters Jesus:

"Jesus entered Jericho and made his way through the town. There was a man there named Zacchaeus. He was the chief tax collector in the region, and he had become very rich. He tried to get a look at Jesus, but he was too short to see over the crowd" (Luke 19:1-3 NLT).

Zacchaeus already had two strikes against him because he was a tax collector, and he was short. Most people know that in this Biblical culture tax collectors were looked at like wicked people; mainly because most of them were. They would cheat the people in their taxes in order to gain money for themselves. Now, something must have been happening inside of Zacchaeus because when he heard that Jesus was coming to his town, something was rising up on the inside of him. He had to see this Jesus. I do not think it is too far-fetched to assume that Zacchaeus may have even heard of a fellow tax collector named Matthew who was now a disciple of Jesus. Perhaps Zacchaeus was at a point in this life where he was desperate for change. Desperate for an encounter with a real God who could rescue him from the life he had been living. He may have a lot of money, but that in no way provides much comfort. Especially when everybody else in the town hates your guts because you gained those riches through deceitful tactics.

"So he ran ahead and climbed a sycamore-fig tree beside the road, for Jesus was going to pass that way" (Luke 19:4 NLT).

I love this. Zacchaeus is so desperate to get a glimpse of this Jesus that he climbs a tree. I am about six feet tall—not super tall, but not super short either. I can tell you, it's hard for me to climb a tree! I am trying to imagine Zacchaeus attempting to climb a tree, and he's so short that this Gospel writer thought it necessary to specify his height challenge. This was so inconvenient. I wonder if Zacchaeus asked anybody around there for a boost to help get him up to the first branch of the tree. If he did, I doubt he received any help because nobody liked him.

Inconvenient.

But when you are desperate for an encounter with the God who can change your circumstances, you will do what it takes to get up that tree.

The NLT and NIV specify that the tree he climbed was a sycamore-fig tree. We learn from Jesus' encounter with Nathanael in John chapter 1 that Nathanael was a man of integrity, which Jesus knew supernaturally. He mentioned that before Philip found him, Jesus had seen him under the fig tree. In Hebraic culture, it was not particularly uncommon for Rabbi's or rabbinical students to spend time in devotion under the fig tree. Though it was indeed literal, it is also an expression for spending time in prayer, worship, and devotion to the Lord. So, it is interesting to me that of all the trees that Zacchaeus could have climbed, he chose to climb a sycamore-fig tree. I believe it a prophetic sign that if you are desperate to get a glimpse of Jesus and you are willing to inconvenience yourself to get it, breakthroughs are inevitable. Climbing that tree of devotion is how you get His attention.

"When Jesus came by, he looked up at Zacchaeus and called him by name. 'Zacchaeus!' He said. 'Quick, come down! I must be a guest in your home today'" (Luke 19:5 NLT).

It is probably safe to say that there were hundreds of people trying to get the attention of Jesus that day…the one who caught Jesus' attention was the one who inconvenienced himself enough to do something radical, even if it was seemingly foolish or difficult to do.

I know ministers who slam other ministries that are run differently than their own, and the only thing they have against that ministry is the fact that they are weird. The fact that they are different. The fact that they are radical or a bunch of tree-climbers. Churches full of poised, convenient, composed people who cannot get the attention of Jesus should not have any argument against a church of radical, inconvenient, and desperate people who draw the gaze of Almighty God. Let's not be weird just to be weird, but when it comes to getting the attention of Jesus, sometimes we will have to do something out of the box in order to stimulate faith out of inconvenience that Jesus simply won't turn a blind eye to.

I ask again: how desperate are you? How hungry are you? What does your climbing-the-mountain-to-get-to-Jesus look like? What does your disregarding the shunning comments of the disciples or the apparent insults of God Himself look like? I know this much, He sees you right where you are, and He is wondering if you are willing to start hiking up that mountainside in order to get to Him, or if you will turn away early and abort your breakthrough. Rest assured, He is praying for you to press on, especially if it's inconvenient.

4
INTIMACY

On August 8th, 2016 I had an encounter with Jesus that has radically changed me. I saw Jesus for the very first time. Now I have seen His works and felt His presence all my life, but I have never actually *seen* Him with my eyes. The encounter came in a dream. The vast majority of the things God speaks to me and the most radical encounters I have with God usually come in dreams. Lots of different things happened in this dream, much of which I still do not understand and some of which I do not feel released to share yet, but there was one key part of the dream I have been sharing whenever possible concerning intimacy.

In the middle of this encounter with Jesus, I suddenly spoke something out of my spirit that the people around me seemed to be incredibly impacted by. I said, "Spending time and intimacy are not the same thing. I could spend time with Ashley playing Yahtzee, but that's not the same as being intimate with her. Jesus is desiring our intimacy, not just our time." When I spoke this out of my spirit in the dream, I knew it was a message from God to me and anybody that would have ears to hear it. This challenged me.

For the next several weeks and months I have been pondering what exactly this means for me. The more I meditated, the more I realized that I do not really know how to be intimate with God. I know how to spend time with Him, but if spending time and being intimate are not the same thing…I am missing something. When I do spend time with the Lord, it is always good, but I can tell it's not best. Kind of like how playing a game with my wife is good, but it's certainly not what I would call intimacy.

So how does one be intimate with God? I started thinking about the times I've had real powerful connections with God in prayer, worship, or in His Word. I could recall times in each of those activities where I felt like I stepped beyond "spending time" and moved into "intimacy" with God. But what was the secret? What shifted my daily Bible reading time to a moment of intimacy? What transforms a time of prayer or worship into an intimate encounter with the Lover of my soul? I still didn't have answers, but I knew that great things worth getting from God do not come quick and easy.

I started paying attention to the moments I felt a real connection with the Lord…when the atmosphere began shifting from a daily discipline to a moment of intimate encounter with King Jesus. I would find myself in casual prayer in the morning when suddenly my mind would shift to something I wasn't expecting to pray for. Perhaps the Spirit of God prompted it, but whatever the topic was, it fit right into my heart. I would be brought to tears or feel an overwhelming sense of His presence. An addictive rush would blow over me as I spent usually just a few seconds engaging from a place of intimacy concerning whatever I was saying in prayer. The same would happen in worship. It could be a song I have heard a thousand times, but suddenly there is a moment where I'm not just *telling* Him He is good and that I love Him, I suddenly feel I'm able to *show* Him I love Him. It is difficult to explain because honestly, I haven't really figured it all out yet. But I know this much, I am convinced that intimacy is different than spending time, and unfortunately most of the church, at best, is giving Him only their time. I would argue that a huge number of Bible believing, church attending, redeemed by the blood of the Lamb, Christians don't have a clue how to be intimate with God.

If you are married, hopefully you're enjoying a wonderful life full of intimacy with your spouse. If you are not married and not being intimate with anybody (as you shouldn't) call up mom and dad and ask them how you got here. Now, without getting too graphic...you know there is a difference between having sex, and being intimate with each other. Anyone can do the very act of having sex; that's not what makes it really special. It is the connection that two married lovers have when being intimate with each other that truly makes it remarkable. When they're being vulnerable with each other. When they're not so much thinking about how they feel, but how they are making the other person feel.

Honestly, this has been the most helpful thought process for me to try to discover how to be intimate with God. What other experiences do I have to pull intimacy from? NONE! What if intimacy with God has some similar ingredients to how I am intimate with my spouse? I'm now learning how to really connect with God when I pray, worship, and study Him...not just to do the acts. I am trying to take the attention off of me and put it on Him. It is not about what I want, what I need, or how I feel, but I am recognizing that I'm called to minister unto the Lord. So maybe I should be far more concerned about how He feels when I'm intimate with Him than me getting through my prayer list or trying to get another touch from Him.

One of the primary duties of the Levitical priests was to minister to God. But everything changed when we stepped into a new covenant with Him.

"But you are not like that, for you are a chosen people. You are royal priests, a holy nation, God's very own possession. As a result, you can show others the goodness of God, for he called you out of the darkness into his wonderful light" (1 Pet. 2:9 NLT).

We are royal priests now! It is up to us to minister unto the Lord. Best part is, we don't minister to the Lord through a myriad of sacerdotal duties like in Old Testament days; rather, we minister to Him out of an expression of what is in our heart—shot like an arrow of adoration into His.

Just connect with your Lover! Be intimate with Him. Connect spirit to Spirit. Be open, honest, and vulnerable with Him. I feel like John hit the nail on the head when he said:

"But the time is coming–indeed it's here now–when true worshipers will worship the Father in spirit and in truth. The Father is looking for those who will worship him that way. For God is Spirit, so those who worship him must worship in spirit and in truth" (John 4:23-24 NLT).

The Church and this nation has got to strive for righteousness in the eyes of the Lord. If we continue to deviate deeper into lawlessness and unrighteousness, the callousness of our hearts concerning our convictions will eventually cover too much of our hearts. I believe such a troubled state could only be remedied by genuine, lasting revival.

A true mark of revival is a fresh appreciation for His manifest presence. His presence is connected to holiness. There's something about His proximity that evaporates our desire for lesser things and we hunger to be like Him. We become what we focus on. He is holy. So when He commands us to be holy as He is holy, we find ourselves in a dilemma. How does one do that? We are to become obsessed with His presence. Intimacy is an expression of gratitude for His presence. His presence purifies. After Yahweh gave instruction on how to make the altar holy and other means of holiness He said, **"I will meet the people of Israel there, in the place made holy by My glorious**

presence" (Ex. 29:43 NLT). The place was made holy by His presence. If it's true for a location, perhaps it's also true for a person. What an incredible thought. His very presence has a way of transforming those into holiness.

Paul tells the Roman church, **"Instead, clothe yourself with the presence of the Lord Jesus Christ. And don't let yourself think about ways to indulge your evil desires" (Rom. 13:14 NLT).** Indulge yourself in things of wickedness, or clothe yourself with the presence of the Lord. They are polar opposites. He is the light of the world. Light simply dispels the darkness. It doesn't have to try to do so, it just does. It destroys it entirely. As we clothe ourselves in the presence of the Lord, we welcome the light of this world to destroy the darkness within.

When referring to forgiveness of sin I've often used the Scripture: **"He has removed our sins as far from us as the east is from the west" (Psa. 103:12 NLT).** I thought it was already amazing enough that our sin was cast as far as east is from west. But after further study, I discovered that the thought is perhaps even more referring to the east—the place where the sun rises. To the west—the place where the sun sets. Light and darkness. When God casts our sin as far as the east is from the west, it's not that if we had a powerful enough telescope we could look east or west far enough and see our sin traveling that direction. Better yet, our sin is obliterated in the same way that light obliterates darkness. It's completely gone! It cannot be found anymore. There is no trace of it.

"For the devious are an abomination to the LORD; But He is intimate with the upright" (Prov. 3:32 NASB).

Continuing to deviate from the Lord will cripple the potential of the Church.

But if we can step into a moral revolution—a righteous thrust of purity and holiness, where Christians actually practice what they preach—a radical intimacy will encounter the Church. Something we clearly need. Then we will see the Bride finally stop attempting to spend time with God at her best, but rather yearn for intimacy with King Jesus unlike never before. This should be the focus of both the corporate Church at large and every individual who calls themselves Christian.

5
PASSIONATE CHRISTIANITY

There's only one way to live out this faith. Passionately. It's practically an oxymoron to consider that Christianity can be lived out without passion. Everything Jesus did flowed from a reservoir of passion for His Father and for humanity. So, if we're to be Christ-like, we absolutely must draw from that same reservoir. Passion is the fuel that should drive our very existence as sons and daughters hungry for the King of Kings. I can recall several scenarios in my short eight years of full-time ministry where I felt overwhelmed, bogged down, discouraged, frustrated, and ready to put my efforts into something else. The temptations of the enemy dangling a big paycheck, a successful business career, or other common pursuits of life in front of me have often looked quite enticing. But this passion—this passionate desire to walk in radical obedience to all God has called me to do—causes all other pursuits to fade away. I have realized that there is nothing else on the face of this earth that I could wholly give myself to and feel this satisfaction that I feel when I know I am doing exactly what God has called me to do. Obedience to His will is everything to me! It's the "sweet spot."

I have a friend named Micah who was doing very well for himself selling hotels in Hawaii. He was newly married to his beautiful bride and had a house on the beach where he could see the perfect break in the waters from lying down in his bed. Livin' the dream you might say! Then one day, the Lord spoke to him to go to Japan to be a missionary. Whoa. Everything was about to change for Micah. He and his wife prayed about it, and separately the Lord confirmed that this was His will by speaking to them both individually to "leave on Friday." This was the confirmation they needed to walk through this door with confidence. They sold all they could, gave away the rest, and bought a plane ticket for Japan. They were full of excitement and wonder! They were being obedient to the will of God, no matter how great the cost.

When they arrived in Japan, upon walking through the airport, fear suddenly gripped Micah. In an instant, this all became *very* real to him. There was another language all over the advertisements on the walls in the terminals. He didn't know where he was going to go because they had no connections with any ministries in Japan. They didn't know where they were going to stay, nor how they were going to get from point A to point B—nothing! He began pondering whether or not he'd made the right decision to randomly leave it all and bring his family to a country he knew nothing about, literally on the other side of the world.

While he was gathering his luggage from baggage claim, he noticed a Japanese man staring at him. He kept looking back at him as they both exchanged glances until Micah concluded that this guy was definitely looking at him with some intention. Micah finally approached the man and said, "Can I help you?"

The man responded in English, "Are you Micah?"

"Yesssssss…"

"This is crazy; I'm a pastor, and I was preparing for our service tonight when the Lord interrupted my study and showed me a vision of your face and told me your name was Micah and that I was supposed to come to this exact baggage claim to find you!" The fear previously clutching Micah was transforming into excitement, praise, and wonder. The radical obedience to God was beginning to pay off. This man ended up providing Micah and his wife with a car, a place to stay, and a location for them to birth their ministry to the Japanese!

Micah told me this story when my wife and I bumped into him and his bride outside of a theatrical play in San Diego. I was moved to my core when I heard the story. He told me, "Josiah, I wouldn't trade the worst day in Japan for the best day in Hawaii...because I was in the 'sweet spot'—the will of God. You know when you're playing basketball, and it just feels like the hoop is 10 times bigger than normal and every time you shoot, it goes in? You practically can't miss! It's because you're in the 'sweet spot.' That's what it's like being in the will of God."

What drives somebody to up and leave everything and go around the world when they have no connections, no direction, no detailed plan, especially when they are seemingly living the American dream on the beach in Hawaii? Passion.

Passion is the thing that provokes athletes to train multiple hours a day, 7 days a week and push their bodies to the limits. Passion is the thing that challenges a love-struck man to chase after the woman who's taking his breath away. Passion is the thing that creatively strikes the heart of a musician or writer to put pen to paper and birth the heartfelt song or book. No doubt, each and every one of us are passionate about something and can understand this to some degree.

Guess where this passion came from?

"Then God said, 'Let Us make man in Our image, according to Our likeness...'" (Gen. 1:26 NKJV).

We are created according to His likeness. In fact, I believe it was His passion for humanity, His creation, that drove Him to create us in the first place. Nothing else He created was made in His image or His likeness. Just us. As beautiful as all of His creation is, we were the ones created out of true passion. No wonder it's passion that marks our existence! No wonder our greatest sense of satisfaction comes from feeding the passion within. He built us this way.

I can remember being passionate about several things when I was younger. Sports, movies, video games, pets, family, relationships, skateboarding; the list goes on and on. Skateboarding was one that probably took the cake above all the rest during my adolescence. Every single day I would tirelessly devote myself to learning new tricks and challenging myself to go big or go home. It certainly had to be passion that would drive me to fly down a flight of stairs, grind a handrail, attempt something crazy or dangerous in hopes to get it captured on film to show my friends. These were before the days of YouTube, but it was quite satisfying to take the footage from my camera, put it onto VHS, and poorly edit it all together in order to show it during lunch time to friends and teachers at school. What little money I had from allowances, birthdays, or Christmases went back into skateboarding. Broken bones, sprains, stitches, concussions—all because I was passionate about something.

Though there are certainly many things we could be passionate about, directing it appropriately toward the One we ultimately received it from in the first place is the best fit for it. His passion for us will always exceed our passion for Him. That's what makes this so beautiful. The more I devote my passionate heart to Him, the more of Him He enables me to experience. The more I know Him, the more I realize how intimately He knows me, which in turn fans the flames of my passion for Him all over again and the cycle continues. When I seek Him in the place of prayer and I realize that He's been waiting in that secret place for me all day, His presence floods my prayer room. Whoa! I love that! When I seek Him in His Word and discover another aspect of His brilliance I never noticed before, my mind is once again blown. Whoa! I love that! When I steer the attention of my heart toward Him in praise and worship and He begins to inhabit the atmosphere created by my passionate worship…whoa!!! I love that!

David says, **"But You are holy, enthroned in the praises of Israel" (Psa. 22:3 NKJV).**

He is holy. He can inhabit whatever He wants to. He is different. He is unlike anybody else, *ever!* But He chooses to sit enthroned in the praises of His people. The praises of the passionate. Our passionate worship creates a throne beckoning the King to be seated upon!

A commonly known verse is Jeremiah 29:11 NKJV, which states, **"For I know the thoughts that I think toward you, says the LORD, thoughts of peace and not of evil, to give you a future and a hope."**

I love that verse, but what speaks to me even more are the following 2 verses**. "Then you will call upon Me and go and pray to Me, and I will listen to you. And you will seek Me and find *Me*, when you search for Me with all your heart" (Jer. 29: 12-13).**

Searching for Him with all of our heart sounds a lot like passionate pursuit to me. It's how we are designed to discover God. Through passion. The passionate heart gains the attention of The Passionate God. That is why when we call upon Him, pray to Him, seek Him…He listens to us and allows Himself to be found by us. We get to love Him because He has first loved us, and now the ball is in our court. We initiate it from here, then He responds. James put it this way, **"Draw near to God and He will draw near to you…" (James 4:8 NKJV).**

We draw near, as He is awaiting for us to do, and then He comes nearer. I have heard it described this way: When you take one step toward Him, you discover that He is actually running toward you. The passionate steps in His direction is what opens our eyes to the understanding of His passionate pursuit of us.

One of my favorite verses in the Bible is 2 Chronicles 16:9 NKJV: **"For the eyes of the LORD run to and fro throughout the whole earth, to show Himself strong on behalf of *those* whose heart *is* loyal to Him…"**

This verse tells me that God is passionately searching throughout the whole earth, looking for a passionate heart dedicated to Him that He can partner with in real intimacy. True love. Yes, this love is between God and that person alone but also so that God can show Himself strong in accomplishing His will in the earth with that person. If it's true that "like spirits attract," then the passionate spirit within us will certainly attract the passionate Spirit of our God. It is then that we discover how we are positioned well to partner with Him for His purposes on the earth.

God, in His holiness, won't typically let us stumble across Him. Now I know that He's sovereign and can do whatever He wants, but in my experience, nobody casually strolls into a church service, casually sings a few songs, casually throws a couple bucks in the offering bag as it goes by, casually listens to the sermon, and then walks out of the building with a life changing experience with Almighty God. Now, things may happen in that service that God can and will use to reach out to an individual in hopes to tug on the heart of that person, inviting them into a passionate relationship with Himself. But for the most part, God is found by those who are truly seeking Him. *God is a Seeker seeking seekers.* His passionate love is looking for the passionate ones to desperately go after Him with all they have.

We should never treat casually the things that God has called holy. His holiness is unparalleled in the universe and that alone merits that we should not treat Him casually. Too often we are guilty of doing this. I am not saying that we cannot come to God in casual conversation and speak to Him face to face like a man speaks to his friend. Nor do we have to approach God with such reverence every time we turn our affections to Him that we can't see Him as a Father but only as a holy distant God, difficult to relate to. This healthy balance is paramount to any believer.

Have you ever heard the story of Uzzah? The book of 1 Samuel states, **"So the men of Kiriath-jearim came to the Ark of the LORD. They took it to the hillside home of Abinadab and ordained Eleazar, his son, to be in charge of it. The Ark remained in Kiriath-jearim for a long time— twenty years in all. During that time all Israel mourned because it seemed the LORD had abandoned them" (1 Sam. 7:1-2 NLT).**

The ark of God was captured by the Philistines and had been in their possession for 20 years. While the ark was in their possession, it was kept at the house of Abinadab. (That information is key to where we're going with this, so keep that in mind). Now, when the Philistines were defeated and David was taking the ark back to Jerusalem, they set the ark on a new cart, which was not supposed to happen in the first place. David should have known that the ark was to be carried on the shoulders of priests, not on a cart. The presence of God was always intended to be carried with you under His directive and plan—not by the convenience or assumptions of those who do not know how to treat the presence of God with reverence and pure worship to begin with.

They placed the Ark of God on a new cart and brought it from Abinadab's house,

which was on a hill. Uzzah and Ahio, Abinadab's sons, were guiding the cart as it left the house, carrying the Ark of God. Ahio walked in front of the Ark. David and all the people of Israel were celebrating before the LORD, singing songs and playing all kinds of musical instruments-lyres, harps, tambourines, castanets, and cymbals. But when they arrived at the threshing floor of Nacon, the oxen stumbled, and Uzzah reached out his hand and steadied the Ark of God. Then the LORD's anger was aroused against Uzzah, and God struck him dead because of this. So Uzzah died right there beside the Ark of God. (2 Sam. 6:3-7 NLT)

Every time I have ever heard this passage preached, this is the part where everybody says, "Awe, poor Uzzah." We always believed that Uzzah was doing the right thing when he reached out to hold up the ark from falling in the dirt. But clearly, God didn't think so. Either God is just mean…or there's something here we are missing. Now, I don't know what would have happened to the ark if Uzzah had let it fall—perhaps it would have floated there supernaturally and then found its way back to the center of the cart. Maybe it would have just fallen to the floor. Who knows? Maybe speculation that the ark was actually going to fall is only assumed because the oxen stumbled would have never actually happened and Uzzah was just looking for an excuse to touch it? I don't know. But one thing is certain, God did not want Uzzah to touch the ark. No matter the circumstances. This was common knowledge amongst the Israelites, in particular the Kohathites or Levites, which Uzzah was (Num. 4:15).

But surely in this instance, that rule could be broken so that the ark of God would not fall to the ground, right? Wrong. For far too long we have made excuses for why we do not have to adhere to the commands of the Lord in full obedience. We are always justifying our actions in order to make us feel better about our sin. The American church I have grown up in is famous for blurring the lines of Scripture or identifying the black and white commands of God to be rather gray. A lesson can be learned here from Uzzah, and I believe the key is found in the fact that he is Abinadab's son. Remember the ark had spent the last 20 years in the house of Abinadab. This tells me that it is very likely that Uzzah grew up around the ark of God. For 20 years, it was in his house. I believe the mistake that Uzzah made was that he became comfortable and casual around something that was always designed to be treated as sacred and holy. "Oh that's just the ark of God. It's just where God lives…right there next to the TV. No big deal." Uzzah's mistreatment of the ark of God, the most sacred item on the face of the earth, especially to his people, is what would cost him his life. His familiarity with the ark of God, over time, diminished his reverence for it.

Today, we find ourselves in much the same boat. Our mistreatment of the presence of God in particular the American church is costing us more than just our physical lives but also our destinies. We casually stroll ourselves into the houses of God, void of passion, and expect God to lavish His overwhelming presence upon us. To grace us with His glory when we gather. To perform miracles in our midst and harken to our beckoning call. Silly Uzzah's. We have been treating the presence of God far too casually, and it's costing us a generation.

Sacred things like leading worship has become about the show and not about the God. Preaching His Word has become more about the personality or the delivery style than the One the message points to. The common elements of a service are driven more by entertainment in hopes to grab the attention of the people and bring them back next week than to grab the attention of God and usher Him back again and again. All of those things are not innately bad, but they dangerously train church-goers to treat that which is holy as casual. Leaders should be working extremely hard to ensure every gathering preserves the reverence of God. No matter the nature of those gatherings.

You may be in the same boat as I was for so many years. Attending church twice a week for decades, expecting God to do the supernatural in my midst but not willing to sacrifice anything for it. My passions were targeted on everything but God, and I had been treating the sacred things of the Kingdom as common. It's no wonder why I was frustrated with my faith. It's no wonder why I could not experience the breakthroughs the depths of my heart yearned for, but I didn't know how to translate those inner desires into a passionate pursuit of the King.

The more people I meet, the more I realize how this Uzzah mindset is plaguing those filling our churches. If you find yourself in the same situation I was in, there is good news for you: passionate repentance can change everything. We need to come to God and repent for walking in the likeness of Uzzah and treating Him like He is not that big of a deal. We would probably never say that with our lips, but our lifestyles scream it loudly enough. Repent from that mindset, change the way we think, and begin passionately pursuing Him in a whole new revelation of His awesomeness and holiness. That honest confession to the Lord is essential if things are ever going to change on the inside of us.

The story of Uzzah is a rather sad one, but I love that it doesn't end there. David, clearly distraught and even upset with the Lord concerning His outburst against Uzzah, decides to put the ark of the covenant in Obed-Edom's house before the journey back to Jerusalem would continue. "Hey Obed, this box just killed somebody who touched it, and we're all kind'ov freaked out by it…we're gonna put it in your house for a while, okay? So, hide your kids, hide your wife…throw the pets outside and make sure you don't touch it, alright!?" The ark remained there for three months, and during that time, Obed-Edom was blessed.

David finally discovered how the ark of the covenant was supposed to be transported—upon the shoulders of the Levitical priests—so he made arrangements to attempt the journey home again with the ark. However, this time he was prepared. This time while on the roughly twelve mile journey to Jerusalem, David offered a sacrifice every six steps in worship to the Lord. He was now rendering reverence and honor to the Lord through his extravagant worship.

After the men who were carrying the Ark of the LORD had gone six steps, David sacrificed a bull and a fattened calf. And David danced before the LORD with all his might, wearing a priestly garment. So David and all the people of Israel brought up the Ark of the LORD with shouts of joy and the blowing of rams' horns. But as the Ark of the LORD entered the City of David, Michal, the daughter of Saul, looked down from her window. When she saw Kind David leaping and dancing

before the LORD, she was filled with contempt for him. (2 Sam. 6:13-16 NLT)

Talk about passion. David danced in reckless, passionate worship before the Lord. He danced before Him. He sacrificed in worship to His name. He let his hair down, set aside his image and reputation, and passionately worshipped the Lord. His own wife was embarrassed of David's abandonment in worship to the Lord, but David did not care. His response to her was amazing: **"So David said to Michal, 'It was before the LORD, who chose me instead of your father and all his house, to appoint me ruler over the people of the LORD, over Israel. Therefore I will play music before the LORD. And I will be even more undignified than this, and will be humble in my own sight...'" (2 Sam. 6:21-22 NKJV).**

Essentially, David was making it very clear that his desires to please the Lord in passionate worship was far more important to him than his image as a king. Furthermore, pleasing his God was more important to him than his own wife's opinion of him. Not that he didn't care about her opinion, but he understood that her opinion of him was secondary in comparison to the Lord's thoughts towards him. How beautiful it is to be married to someone whose primary desire in life is to enhance and encourage your relationship with the Lord first and foremost. Yet, frustrating can be the marriage where a spouse does not understand that most important relationship of all is their personal relationship with the Lord and second to that, their spouse's relationship with the Lord. Appropriating our passions to the King of Kings as a priority will set us up for success in any relationship we find ourselves in. Your goal in every relationship is to encourage that other person's relationship with the Lord. Period.

I want to give you permission to live passionately. What do you think that means for you? A passionate lifestyle to you may look differently than what it does for me, but that is not the point. The goal here is to understand where you are at and where you want to be in your relationship with the Lord. I would not pretend to think that everybody desires to live a full, maturing, passionate Christian life. Some people just want their fast-food Jesus, their casual church, their powerless, passionless so-called Christianity and barely make it into Heaven by the skin of their teeth just as long as they make it there. To which I am both sad and frustrated to admit that this mindset is swallowing those within our churches today in America.

We want the blessings of God but are unwilling to change the way we live. We can't bathe in blessings while swimming in curses. Refusing to repent from the things that quench our relationship with the Lord and disarm our passion only continue to muddy the waters. True, authentic repentance cleanses us by the blood of Jesus so we can be positioned to receive His magnificent blessings. This fosters the passionate lifestyle. This protects the beneficial hunger each of us needs to joyfully fan the flame burning within us. In fact, I would dare to say that the greatest blessings from God are the blessings that provoke us to repentance. When Peter was addressing the religious leaders while on trial in the temple he said, **"When God raised up his servant, Jesus, he sent him first to you people of Israel, to bless you by turning each of you back from your sinful ways" (Acts 3:26 NLT).** The blessing was connected to turning from sinful ways. This makes a lot of sense when the scope of eternity is in mind. You could be blessed with every kind of earthly blessing you can think of, but if sin has your heart, not Almighty God, none of it will matter when we die.

How many dreams and destinies are laid unclaimed out there? How many people just want to make it into Heaven in hopes to escape the tortures of hell but don't care about Heaven on earth or the will of God for their lives? I hope that is not you. If it is, there is still good news: repentance and asking God to fill you with a passionately obedient love for Him can change everything. After wholeheartedly repenting to God, it's time to start mapping out some simple things that you can begin to do on a daily basis in order to fuel the flames of fiery passionate abandonment to our King.

Obviously, I don't know your story. You might be hurting so badly from past experiences to even consider living passionately for much of anything. My pastor, Brian Ross, once said, "Passion propels us through the pain". If we are passionate enough, we will discover a surfacing strength to endure more than perhaps we ever thought we could. He further explained that both passion and pain have the same root word. There will always be a connectivity to the passionate lifestyle and pain. Obedience to God is not always cake and ice cream. Sometimes it means you are persecuted. It often means laying down some things that we want or worked hard for. That is rarely a comfortable experience. But passion can propel you through the pain if you will not give up. It's no wonder the crucifixion of Jesus is also called the Passion of Christ. In the greatest dispensation of passion, we see a great deal of pain. But His passion propelled Him through it.

It's time to live a lifestyle of passionate worship. It's time to seek God in the place of prayer. It's time to devour His Word. It's time to begin talking with family and friends about the things God is doing in our lives and what He desires for them. It's time to share our testimony with those who will listen. It's time to stop warming the seats of our churches and begin serving at a greater capacity. It's time to mend our broken relationships. It's time to pursue righteousness unlike ever before. It's time to further our education and knowledge of our God. The list can go on and on, so whatever you decide to do, just do something! The satisfaction of a lifetime is awaiting you. It's a satisfaction that can only be discovered in the laid-down life of the passionate ones, wildly in love with King Jesus! This is the passionate life we're all called to live. So go for it!

6
Don't Be Such a Baby

I feel called of God to help mature those God has given me stewardship over. Discovering your calling can be a difficult thing, but it doesn't have to be. Some of the best advice I've been given was to follow what breaks my heart or the things that frustrate me. I may be called to tackle that very thing. So, I did. Something that both breaks my heart and frustrates me is seeing immature Christians with little fruit and practically no growth who have been in the church perhaps their whole lives. It both drives me crazy and brings me to tears.

One of the responsibilities of any parent is to mature their children. To graduate them from an infancy stage, to a toddler stage, to an adolescent stage, then eventually adulthood. Often their success in the world is determined by how we mature our children at a young age. I feel this same sense of responsibility for the church. When my wife and I first came to where I am currently pastoring young adults, we started working with a small group of young adults who were very churched but not very mature. The simple things of the Kingdom were foreign to them. Even though most of them had grown up in the church their entire lives. They had several stories about camps, trips, people, events, and so on, but couldn't tell me where to find a particular book of the Bible, pray consistently, lead somebody to the Lord or show me any real fruit. What were we to do?

Start at square one.

My wife and I started teaching these some twenty to thirty year church attenders the basics of Christianity. You'd think it was redundant or boring to them but it was quite the opposite. What should have been review was in fact revelatory. In all honesty, it wasn't that they were hearing these things for the first time, though sometimes that was the case; it was more that they were now ripe and accountable to grow unlike ever before. We made sure they understood our purpose was to grow them by the help of the Holy Spirit. We were demanding fruit of them. They knew and felt that we loved them and didn't want to see another several decades go by where they remained on the same cycle of dysfunction and fruitlessness. Healthy things grow. They were obviously not growing, therefore obviously not healthy.

Paul put it like this:

"When I was a child, I spoke and thought and reasoned as a child. But when I grew up, I put away childish things" (1 Cor. 13:11 NLT).

We have got to stop being such spiritual babies and grow up. There are so many Christians who've been walking with the Lord year after year, and they are still sucking on pacifiers, and it's getting weird. Spiritual moms and dads have got to begin to demand that their spiritual sons and daughters grow up and put away childish things. It is a bold thing to place demands on the people within our congregations because in our American churches there is a majority of congregants who don't want anything demanded of them. Like we've talked about in previous chapters, they feel like they're doing the pastor a favor by even attending church. Why in the world would they want something demanded of them spiritually when they are at church? Church is supposed to make them feel good right? To whom much is given much is required. So, if church goers continue to fly under the radar by not receiving much, then not much will be required of them. If they are given many spiritual deposits for growth, then they are demanded to grow and demanded to bear fruit which has been His plan from the beginning.

Unfortunately, our land is plagued with churches who won't place these demands on people because it makes them feel uncomfortable. They'd rather get them to come back next week as churches continue to spoon feed them baby food while we tally them up on our attendance records. So, we may have thousands in attendance, but it's actually a slap in the face to the Kingdom of God to have thousands of babies in attendance who continue to remain immature and bear no fruit. Far better is the church with dozens in attendance and active spiritual maturity than the contrary.

I think this was Jesus' game plan as well. Focus on a few that He knew He could mature. He didn't attempt to mature the multitudes. He would just get disappointed. He could sprinkle a little nourishment onto a massive field, or water well a small garden that had the capacity to multiply over time into a massive harvest. He knew what would stand the test of time and ultimately flip the world upside down. I think we should follow His model.

I think many churches have got it backwards. We attempt to grow numerically in hopes to then grow those large numbers spiritually. If we would focus our efforts in spiritually growing those already committed to our churches, the natural byproduct of their maturity will be numerical growth. However, growth takes time. Sometimes, longer than we're willing to wait. Real maturity isn't measurable without some degree of longevity. People cannot help but tell others what is working for them. The best multi-level marketing businesses I've come across are the ones where nobody nags me about the business; I more or less stumble across them because I can see the obvious transformation in an individual. What I see working for someone makes me inquisitive. I have family members that are physically shrinking right now due to shedding amazing amounts of unwanted weight, and they didn't go around telling everybody about their business opportunity. The fruit of the product and their commitment to it simply speaks for itself. People who know them see the very noticeable difference and start asking questions. The same will occur for the Church when individuals start becoming more like Christ as they mature — when they start seeing the Bible lived out before their very eyes. When the promises of God within these Scriptures start happening in their day-to-day lives. That's an invite far more appealing to people than any promotional flyer is. I am not against promotions at all. I think we should do all that we can to see the church grow. I just don't want to sacrifice Biblical Christianity and the demands of God to mature on the altar of numerical success. The Church should be growing numerically, just the right way. I know lots of churches that have incredible numerical success, but I wouldn't call their congregation mature. Like a baby with a beard, there are things that look mature but in reality, they aren't.

Chuck Smith, founder of Calvary Chapel, once shared some incredible insight on the topic. He was raised believing that the primary purpose of the Church was to evangelize the world. Although he knew he wasn't an evangelist, he believed evangelization of the world is what the Church should be doing. So, he would often share evangelistic messages with little fruit in return, all the while feeling a bit out of his element. He was very comfortable as a pastor/teacher but not an evangelist. Chuck Smith had a revelation from the Lord that the primary purpose of the Church, in particular the five-fold ministry, was not to evangelize the world but rather to build up the body of Christ.

Ephesians 4:11-12 NLT says, **"Now these are the gifts Christ gave to the church: the apostles, the prophets, the evangelists, and the pastors and teachers. Their responsibility is to equip God's people to do his work and build up the church, the body of Christ."**

So this is exactly where Pastor Chuck Smith shifted his efforts to. He started pouring more and more into the body of Christ. As a result, the body got healthier and more mature. As their maturity developed, their lives became a witness to the world around them. People started noticing the Christ-likeness manifesting in the lives of Christians. Evangelism was the natural byproduct of a healthy church body.

Please don't misunderstand me and think that because your primary gifting is not an evangelist that you shouldn't lead people to the Lord. That's not what I'm saying at all. We should all *do the work of an evangelist* and *he who wins souls is wise*. Still, I can relate with Pastor Chuck Smith. I have a heart for the Church, and though I love to see souls saved, I know evangelism is not my gifting. But, if I do my part in helping mature the evangelists that God has called to run alongside me, the lost will be swept into the Kingdom. This enables me to move in my gifting and strengths which equips others in maturity so they can move in their gifting and strengths. Everybody wins!

I have a friend named Ryan who loves to minister to people everywhere he goes. He's constantly buying food for people on the streets and loving on the world around him. He has led people to the Lord and seen miracles break out in many unconventional locations. He has a gift for this that I simply don't have. It's not that I can't, I have done some of the same. But his spiritual gifting in this area produces fruit with ease where mine tends to come with much more effort and strife. However, my sweet spot is by helping to mature guys just like him. In fact, Ryan has always been extremely vocal about when he started coming to our young adult ministry years ago and how his faith finally started maturing. After a lifetime of infantile faith, he's now more mature than ever. Now, he's able to bless the world around him through his lifestyle. So what should I do to reach the world? Keep striving to evangelize on the streets? Perhaps, as the Spirit leads. But, I'm seeing that I'm far more effective to reach those on the streets through Ryan than I am by personally going. That may shift in the future as the Lord gives grace, but for now, I see the fingerprint of God on this strategy.

When you are walking closely with the Father, your heart begins to beat in sync with His. I doubt that when the greatest Dreamer of all dreamed up my life He dreamt it to be mediocre. I'm sure he wanted me to make minimum wage, have an okay family, with an okay marriage, in an okay church, doing some okay things for God in an okay city. Somehow I doubt that. It's still true that He said:

"I know the plans I have for you," says the LORD. "They are plans for good and not for disaster, to give you a future and a hope" (Jer. 29:11 NLT).

God absolutely has dreamt up some amazing things for us. This verse is probably the most popular verse in American Christianity right now. It is on every mug, decorative piece, sticker, Bible cover, and T-shirt where I live. But this verse only deals with God's part. It's about what He's doing—His plans for us. We love to talk about what His part is because, once again, it removes us from any responsibility to mature and take any action into our own hands. Take a look at the next two verses.

"In those days when you pray, I will listen. If you look for me wholeheartedly, you will find me" (Jer. 29:12-13 NLT).

When we pray. There's already an assumption that we should be praying. Something the immature Christian doesn't really do, unless they find themselves in a crisis. Secondly, we need to be looking for Him with all of our hearts, then we will find Him. There's a big IF there. Immature believers are unfortunately not looking for Him with all of their hearts. They're looking for Him casually on Sundays at 10:00am. They're looking for Him casually when they like their friends' social media posts. If they're on another level then maybe they're looking for Him at a midweek service as well. But I would argue that most are not looking for Him with all of their hearts. If that is true, then we are not holding up our end of this conditional promise. No wonder we can't seem to find Him. We are not looking for Him with all of our hearts. So we are finding church but never God. We find fresh coffee but no spiritual maturity. We discover great music, but no act of true worship. We uncover relationships with others in place of our relationship with Him.

I would dare to say that the plans that He has for our lives, the plans for good, not for disaster, to give us a future and a hope will not come to pass if we don't pray, and search for Him wholeheartedly. A lifestyle of seeking Him and intimacy will deposit within us a heart that beats rhythmically with His. Jeremiah 29:11 is not a fluffy feel good Scripture to help get us through another day. Some of us have always seen it that way. It's a challenging, lifestyle provoking Scripture that beckons us to take the call of God seriously enough to seek Him with all our hearts till the day we die. Print that on your coffee mug.

Mature Christians have some form of healthy vision. When they mature, they gain the vision of God for their lives and the plans and purposes of God for the world around them. That Jeremiah 29:11 promise begins to take on skin and bone. But once again, notice that this vision comes to the mature. I believe God entrusts His plans and purposes into the lives and hearts of believers who will do something with what He's entrusted to them. He is not wasteful.

I have heard it taught that when Elijah told Elisha, "If you see me when I'm taken up then you'll have what you're asking for." The more literal translation is "If you see what I see when I'm taken up then you'll have what you're asking for." In other words, Elijah is saying if you've walked closely enough with me to not only be near in proximity to me, but to inherit my vision, you'll be able to have this difficult thing you're asking for, because you can be trusted with it.

Shortly after this, a chariot of fire comes to separate them and a whirlwind takes Elijah up to Heaven while Elisha sees the whole thing. I imagine the same principle applies to us in relation to Almighty God. If we can walk closely enough to Him by maturing into the sons and daughters He's called us to be, we'll inherit His vision for the earth. This is what we need. We all ought to mature to the point where we can be trusted with His vision for our lives and the lives of those around us. His vision will always be far grander than our own.

All my life I have been in churches where the senior pastor constantly tried to share his vision for the church to the people. Everything that happened within the church was in response to his vision. I've been blessed to be under some great men of God who got their vision from Heaven concerning where God was taking the church, so they were worthy visions to follow, but it got me thinking. I knew as I matured in my relationship with the Lord, I was supposed to serve the vision of another person if God was ever going to give me a vision of my own. But even while I was serving their visions, God was stirring up so many things inside me that I yearned to see. I knew God had called me to that specific ministry for that specific season so I wasn't planning to run off and go chase these dreams elsewhere to make them happen prematurely. That did not feel like wisdom or maturity. Still, I thought the right thing to do was to let those dreams and visions sit dormant until one day God would awaken them. My vision was never to compete with the vision of those I was serving. My allegiance to the call of God to serve the vision of that pastor only better positions me to one day be released into my own.

Here is what I am learning now: if God has truly called me to run alongside someone in ministry, then the vision He's built into my heart will complement the vision of theirs. Now I'm not only serving their vision, but I feel a radical sense of ownership for their vision. When I've matured to the point where God has entrusted His vision to me, I find that my personal God-dreamt plans and dreams for my life compliment those I've been called to run alongside with. The two visions fit together, and now I'm sharing in the equity that comes from pressing forward both in my personal vision and the vision of those I'm running with.

Instead of always trying to get others to buy into my vision, I endeavor to mature those running with me to gain a vision of their own. As they mature, if they are truly called to run with me, their vision and my vision will fit together like two pieces of a puzzle. That is priceless. Attempting to get others to adopt your vision as their own is extremely difficult, just ask almost any pastor. It's not too difficult to find others to serve your vision but for them to fight for it through thick and thin as if it was their own baby is no simple task. But when they've matured and now carry a vision of their own that compliments the vision God has given you, then every time they invest in their own vision they are in turn investing in yours as well. Now they'll fight for it through thick and thin because it really is their baby. Both parties have their own visions from God, birthed in the heart of God and then planted in the hearts of individuals who are willing to grow together until they see the fulfillment of these God given dreams come to pass. Once again, a prerequisite to the success of this revelation is individual maturity. Advancement moves from addition to multiplication quickly and each contributor sows sacrificially into their own visions. Literally, everybody wins!

Damon Thompson, the man who has probably invested more into my life from a distance than anybody on the planet, once said, "Maturity is not the occasional application of extraordinary things, rather it is the consistent application of elementary things." I admit I would often be impressed by the guest speaker who would blow in, blow up, blow out. Their gifting was often impressive. The anointing that seemed to be upon them was exciting. The atmosphere was always electric and the people always came with great expectation. I thought these people were so mature. Many of them were, but many of them were not. As time went on, the true colors of several would be revealed and let's just say their behavior was not that of a mature Christian. The extraordinary things they were doing in revival style services was not a display of maturity.

I've also known several amazing old saints of God who have served Him faithfully year after year doing the fundamental things of the Kingdom with the flame of love still burning deep within them. I'm not talking about learning *only* the elementary things of the Kingdom and not advancing beyond that as the writer of Hebrews warns us not to do (Heb.6:1-3). I'm referring to maintaining a discipline of spiritual maturity that doesn't look like a momentarily exciting firework but more like a constant growing flame. I want to be like the mature ones all the days of my life. They spend time in His Word every day. They worship and pray every day. They serve their churches, communities, and spouses. Perhaps they don't get many accolades for how they live, but because they are mature, they don't need any. They are not looking for the approval of man nor the applause of the church. Their interest is in pleasing Almighty God as they fall deeper in love with Him, and so they consistently apply the elementary things of the Kingdom as a lifestyle.

To me, that is what maturity looks like. That is what we should all be striving for. So, hear the word of the Lord to many of us today: don't be such a baby. It's time to mature into the son or daughter He's calling you to be. Grow. Really grow. Consistently apply the elementary things of the Kingdom every day of your life. You can do this. With the help of the Holy Spirit, you-can-do-this.

7
COVENANT

Our understanding of a covenant is minimal compared to authentic Biblical covenants. The covenantal agreement or promise between two parties was a commitment neither would dare break. Today, when we accept Jesus Christ as Lord and Savior—experiencing salvation—we enter into a covenant with Him. A covenant written and sealed in the precious blood of Jesus. In a nutshell, here's the covenant: We were on our way to hell, Jesus paid the price we could never pay to free us from that damnation, and now we belong to Him forever. He gets ALL of us. Not a portion of us. Not us on Sundays at 10:00am or when we pray before a meal. All of us. That's the true covenantal agreement we sign when we accept Him not only as Savior, but as Lord of our lives.

When God made a covenant with Abraham, the father of the faith, He gave Abraham a mark of the covenant. Circumcision. When males were circumcised it was a sign that they were covenant people. They belonged to the Lord.

Then God said to Abraham, "Your responsibility is to obey the terms of the covenant. You and all your descendants have this continual responsibility.
This is the covenant that you and your descendants must keep: Each male among you must be circumcised.
You must cut off the flesh of your foreskin as a sign of the covenant between me and you.
From generation to generation, every male child must be circumcised on the

eighth day after his birth. This applies not only to members of your family but also to the servants born in your household and the foreign-born servants whom you have purchased.
All must be circumcised. Your bodies will bear the mark of my everlasting covenant." (Gen. 17:9-13 NLT)

When God chose where this mark of the covenant was going to happen on the body, I don't think He just chose some random private part for no apparent reason. Circumcision takes place on the male's body at the point of contact where life is given through reproduction. For the Israelites, every time two married people were intimate with each other, they had this reminder of the covenant they were in with the Lord. This was what God intended. A way of communicating that every bit of life that comes forth from this intimacy these two people share with each other comes forth with the covenant blessing of God in mind. Whatever generations would come as a consequence of intimacy with each other was going to come through the covenant. Literally, it would flow through the covenant sign of obedience and consecration to God.

It's not enough for us to offer God lip service. We can't show up to church, pay our tithe, serve when there's a need and go through all the motions if we never really enter into covenant relationship with Him. Covenant takes things to a whole new level.

When we enter into covenant with Him we get His name:

"You shall not take the name of the LORD your God in vain, for the LORD will not hold him guiltless who takes His name in vain" (Ex. 20:7 NKJV).

My whole life I thought that meant, don't swear using His name or you will be in big trouble. Though I agree that is a good idea not to do that, the truth goes deeper. When we enter into covenant relationship with Almighty God, we take on His name as a bride takes on her husband's name when she gets married to him. My wife's maiden name was Ashley Jane Ewing, now it's Ashley Jane Elias. She's taken on my name. Ashley Elias is now her legal name and she has access to everything I own. We are equal partners in this marriage and all that I have belongs to her and all that she has belongs to me. In fact, when there is something we don't want to share with each other and the other person wants it, we will play the "One Flesh/Marriage" card and try to get it that way. She always takes my cookies this way.

When we were married, we gave each other tokens of our love and devotion to one another. They are signs and symbols of the covenant we were making: our wedding rings. They are meant for everybody to see so the world knows that she belongs to me, and I belong to her. Giving the rings to each other was a pleasure, not a formality. Signing the marriage certificate wasn't what made our marriage legitimate, just like praying the prayer wasn't what made our salvation legitimate. It was the motive behind the covenant we were making one with another and likewise with God through faith.

When that covenant is lived out, it is a wonderful representation of the God we serve. People see Jesus through our marriage. Sometimes I feel like a greater display of worship during a worship service is to have my arms upon my wife's shoulders instead of lifted in the air. My love displayed toward her in that moment is a form of worship and warfare. I have often had people come up to me after services and tell me how they are watching my family and me, and it blesses them so much to see how we love each other.

I remember once being on a long drive back to San Diego from Utah. We were passing through San Bernardino when my pregnant wife had a sudden craving for Taco Bell. We don't normally eat Taco Bell, but that was one of the things she craved while pregnant so we had it often during those 9 months. When pregnant wife wants something…you get it for her! So, her pregnant senses kicked in, and she miraculously spotted a Taco Bell off the side of the freeway. I didn't see it, but I assumed she knew what she was talking about. Pregnant women have super powers…I don't know how else to say it. We exited the freeway, made a left, and looked for the Taco Bell. It was nowhere in sight. So we drove for a little bit looking for it and couldn't spot it. Then we had to make it official and find it in our GPS. It turned out this Taco Bell was about 3 miles in the opposite direction through side streets. Now I'm getting a little frustrated that preggo over here had to have her Taco Bell and didn't tell me it was miles in the opposite direction, extending our already super long drive. I was trying to keep my cool. There were several moments where I wanted to say some unproductive things, but knowing that we still had several hours in the car together, it probably wasn't the wisest idea. So I kept my mouth shut. (There's a revelation right there for any husbands paying attention. It could save your marriage, or if she's pregnant, save your life. Keep your mouth shut.)

We both kept our cool with each other and kept smiles on our faces. When we arrived at Taco Bell and sat down to eat, we noticed a guy in the corner watching us. We were in a somewhat sketchy part of town, so I was keeping him in the corner of my eye while we ate. Suddenly, he spawned conversation with us out of nowhere. He was admiring my family from a distance. He told me how blessed I must be to have such a beautiful family. Out of nowhere he asked me if I would pray for him. He told me that he wanted what I have and whatever I'm doing I need to keep on doing it. I never once told him I was a Christian or even hinted towards it. Apparently we were just radiating Jesus in there while slamming down chalupas. He further explained that he was waiting for his wife to meet him there at that Taco Bell. They were currently separated but not divorced, and she was meeting with him there to discuss their situation. He was hopeful that they were going to work out their problems and get back together. My wife Ashley jumped on the opportunity and began praying for him. She didn't hold anything back and prayed bold, powerful, Spirit-led prayers and even prophesied over him right inside Taco Bell. It was a radical God moment for each of us.

As we drove away we realized that we had a choice when we were on our adventure trying to find Taco Bell whether we were going to let our frustrations get the best of us and lash out at each other or not. Because we chose to keep our emotions under control, we exemplified an intact covenant relationship between the two of us which was exactly what this guy needed to see. The two of us walking out our covenant in love and patience with each other was prophesying hope to him for his marriage. We will surely never know the extent of the eyes that are on us and perhaps the spotlight the Lord will shine upon our covenant relationships. Therefore, we have got to be intentional about strengthening and protecting our covenant relationships with each other. This doesn't mean we never fight. This doesn't mean we don't have bad days. This means we do everything within our power to keep our covenant laced with love intact.

When we enter into covenant with the Lord and we don't walk in the calling, honor, reverence, righteousness, and power that comes through that covenant; I believe we're taking His name in vain. Taking His name in vain is not simply swearing while using His name…it's living way below the standard any bride of the Bride-Groom should be living when their Husband is King of the universe. Taking the Lords name in vain is calling yourself a Christian but living like the devil. It's claiming the name of Christ, but living like that name you carry is not a big deal. I believe it breaks God's heart, just like it would break my heart if my wife married me and then treated our marriage like it was not a big deal. If she lived like the covenant we made and the vows we shared with each other were merely just words, having no power or heart motivating it, that would hurt. Much like how it would hurt the Lord to treat our covenant with Him so carelessly.

I would love to encourage you to evaluate your salvation experience. Did you enter into a covenant with the Lord or did you just pray a prayer in hopes to get out of hell? Going to Heaven is an amazing thing, but if our motive on earth is *only* to get to Heaven and escape hell, we are missing the whole motive behind why He paid the price to get us into Heaven. It is because He loves us so passionately, that He can't stand to spend an eternity without us. He has made a way where there was no way so that our love for each other can accelerate for an eternity. Then He established a covenant with us to prove how serious He is about His love for us and sealed it with the Holy Spirit, the Promise that He's coming again for His bride. While we wait for His return, we get to enjoy relationship with Him here on earth. Don't wait to get to Heaven to be with Jesus; be with Him today! If the decision you made to accept Jesus into your life as Lord and Savior was with any other motive other than covenant, passionate, fiery love with Him and gratefulness for the wonderful gift of freedom He offered you, then make a fresh commitment today to come into covenant with Him. Making that fresh commitment in covenant to Him will renew a flame of love on the inside of you. Don't let another day go by outside of authentic covenantal relationship with Him. If you need to do that, then be bold, humble, and honest; and do it. I did.

8
Who Is Here Among You?

There's an interesting story that comes out of Numbers chapter eleven. Israel was wandering through the desert, and the people were complaining. Their complaints were frustrating both God and Moses. Foreigners living amongst the Israelites were reminiscing of times back in Egyptian captivity. They remembered that although they were slaves, they had food to eat other than the manna which they had been eating every day and were getting sick of. The complaints of the foreigners were contagiously affecting the Israelites who were then beginning to complain themselves. They all started whining and crying out for meat. God's response to Moses who was ready to give up on these whining people was this:

> **And say to the people, "Purify yourselves, for tomorrow you will have meat to eat. You were whining, and the LORD heard you when you cried, 'Oh, for some meat! We were better off in Egypt!' Now the LORD will give you meat, and you will have to eat it. And it won't be for just a day or two, or for five or ten or even twenty. You will eat it for a whole month until you gag and are sick of it. For you have rejected the LORD, who is here among you, and you have whined to him, saying, 'Why did we ever leave Egypt?'" (Num. 11:18-20 NLT)**

Just when we thought we knew what we wanted, this story reminds us that we probably have no clue what we really want, but our Father in Heaven knows best. God is going to give them what they wanted in such abundance it's going make them sick! This punishment is coming their way because they have rejected the LORD, Who is there among them, and not to mention the whining. I would like to capitalize on the fact that God was there among them while all of this was happening. Here is the reason why.

His nearness to us blows my mind. His accessibility is hard to fathom. All I have to do is close my eyes and turn my attention to Him, and I can converse with the Almighty God. He is so close! I think on Him and there He is. He is so approachable, even in His awesome power and majesty, He is beckoning me to come spend time and be intimate with Him. It should clearly be the other way around, but for some reason He wants to be with me far more than I want to be with Him.

I believe it was evangelist Reinhard Bonnke who said, "In all other religions man seeks God. In the Christian faith, God seeks man." It is so backwards. We should be the ones begging at His feet for scraps of attention; instead, He is jealous for our attention as we so lavishly distribute it to the world. So He patiently waits and continues to call us to draw nearer to Him. UNBELIEVABLE!

The Israelites were certainly in the wrong for their complaining, especially about going back to Egypt, the place from which God had so dramatically delivered them. I cannot imagine why anybody would desire the choice foods of captivity when they get to eat the Frosted Flakes (manna) of freedom. But the greater sin in my opinion was their obvious neglect of Yahweh Himself Who was right there among them. They were disregarding the presence of the God manifested there with them. Apparently they were getting a little too comfortable with God in their midst that they started treating Him like He was not that big of a deal.

We have already learned about Uzzah's mistake for not treating the ark of God like a big deal in the Passionate

Christianity chapter. His story fits well here. Spending 20 years with the ark can get you pretty accustomed to it, where all of a sudden, the sacredness of it begins to fade. Perhaps this is what was happening to the people of Israel. Thinking with their bellies instead of remembering all that God had done for them.

Here in America, we are so wildly privileged. In this very moment, I can effortlessly access so much content concerning the Bible. I can also walk into thousands of different churches all throughout the land and listen to a Gospel presentation from incredible preachers and teachers. I can feel free to worship my God openly with my personal expression of praise without fear of being persecuted for my faith. I can listen to the most sought after preachers of our day in a moment's time. I click a button and have their books, teachings, apparel, study guides, and who knows what else in an instant or at my door step within a day or two. We have got it all, and yet in the midst of all we have I think many of us have forgotten Who is here among us.

Perhaps our options and liberties have spoiled us so greatly we are gagging on quail meat. We've been enjoying stuffing our faces with everything about Him that we never realized His displeasure in our missing Him. We have fallen in love with church, worship, pastors, programs, lights, music, the Bible, small groups, and every other accompanying thing but in the mess, missed Him. It's pointless to go to church if you are going to miss Him in the midst of it. It's pointless to step into a worship service and start singing songs if you miss the One you ought to be worshipping. It's pointless to read The Book and miss the Author. All of those things are wonderful, but they are meant to draw us to Him. They are wonderful tools that He has given us and privileged us to be able to enjoy so that we can know Him. I don't just want to know the Bible, I want to love on the Author! The more I fall in love with the Author, the more I'll fall in love with His best-seller love letter to me, the Bible! We need a radical recalibration of what this is all about; it's about Him, and He is here among us.

Many of us still think we need another thing in order to get connected to Him. We need to hear another message, get another prophetic word, buy another Bible, get slain in the Spirit once more, get another autograph, sing another song before we'll really connect with Him, and IT'S NOT WORKING! What I feel the Spirit of God is beckoning us to do is stop all of that nonsense, close our eyes, and engage with Jehovah Shammah, The Lord Who is there. He is present. He is with you as you read this book in this very moment. He is with me while I type this out in my living room. He is here. Even if you feel like you don't deserve Him to be there, He's still there, because He's just that good. It doesn't matter the things that you have been wrestling with, trying to overcome, struggling day in and day out over. Shut it all down, and just engage with Him in the quiet of the moment you are currently in. It is there you'll discover He's waiting for you. Let me provoke you to rekindle the flame of devotional passion with the King of Kings Who so passionately loves you. May I remind you, Who is here among you.

9
EBENEZER

In recent years, I have made a great effort to record and remember all that God is doing in my life. It wasn't long ago when I realized I was being a bad steward of recalling and celebrating what the Lord was doing in my life. I celebrated my moments of breakthrough in that moment but failed to continue to celebrate what God had done in my past. Only some of the testimonies would I remember but surely not all of them. I had fallen victim to Christian amnesia. When I converse with people within the church, it's not uncommon for them to say how good God is and yet, when I ask what specifically God is doing in their lives there is often an awkward pause. We know God is good and doing good things, but we can't recall any of them. That's a problem. If we don't steward and celebrate well the activity of God in our lives, then the activity will cease.

Working in the church means I hear a lot of testimonies because God is doing a lot. If we're not careful, testimonies will become mundane or even disinteresting. I've been there. When we pray for somebody with a need, the goal is for that need to turn into a testimony. That means, somehow, some way, God stepped in and did something. The salvation manifested. The healing took place. The breakthrough happened. That's what we were hoping for the moment we started praying in the first place, right? Otherwise why pray at all? So, why do we often feel so invested in the prayer yet disconnected from the answer? Are we praying for others because it's the right thing to do, but we really don't expect God to actually do anything? Needless to say, something in all of this was wrong.

I've recently challenged myself to truly celebrate the testimonies I'm hearing. Every time I hear a testimony of something I want God to do again in the life of another or in my personal life, I stop everything and celebrate through thanksgiving to God for at least thirty seconds to a minute. That may seem small, but after doing it the first time I realized how little I previously honored the activity of God. Thanking Him for thirty seconds to a minute seemed like forever. But the more I do it, the more I condition my inner man to expect the activity of God. I'm teaching my soul what to honor. I'm displaying what I value. I'm celebrating the very thing I want to happen again and again.

The Israelites had this same problem. It wasn't long after plagues devastated Egypt, fire came from Heaven, seas parted, water poured forth from a rock and so many more wondrous signs occurred that Israel appears to have forgotten what Yahweh was recently and even presently doing. Our culture is much the same concerning this problem. We always want a fresh word, a fresh encounter, a fresh message…something new, something new, something new, and we so quickly forget what God did in our lives yesterday. Though I agree that it is incredibly important to be forward thinking and always yearning for what God has for us today and tomorrow, I think it is a grievous error to forget what He did yesterday.

There are many accounts of God-fearing people building altars, naming places, naming children, erecting memorials and many other things in order to remember the activity of God. Let's look at one wonderful account of this.

Israel was in battle against the Philistines, and they were losing. Then they had the brilliant idea to take the ark of the covenant from the Most Holy Place out to the battle with them hoping the Lord would give them victory over the Philistines. The people were so excited when the ark of God arrived on the battlefield that the troops shouted so loud the ground shook. The Philistines heard the roar from the soldiers of Israel and instead of tucking their tail between their legs in fear, they stood their ground and fought all the more. Now, because God never directed Israel to bring the ark to the battlefield, there was no favor in battle for them and thirty thousand Israelite soldiers died that day as they suffered defeat. All this took place at a location called "Ebenezer." Ebenezer means "stone of help." The ark of God was captured by the Philistines, and while it was in Philistine possession, God wreaked havoc upon the Philistines to the point that they were desperate to get rid of it. When it was returned, it was not returned to the Most Holy Place where it belonged, and for twenty years it was displaced. That is a long time since the battle at Ebenezer. That is a long time for the loss of the ark to sink into the hearts of the people. In fact, 1 Samuel 7:2 NLT records, **"...During that time all Israel mourned because it seemed the LORD had abandoned them."**

Such a long period of time had passed that the people were beginning to think that the Lord had abandoned them. Whenever they thought about the name "Ebenezer," I'm sure there was a terrible taste in their mouths. Then, the prophet Samuel inspired a revival in the hearts of the people, and they got rid of everything that had been keeping them from God, and they all attended a prayer meeting at Mizpah. While they were there praying and confessing their sins, word got to the Philistines that all of Israel had gathered at one location, so they mobilized their armies against the Israelites there.

Could you imagine attending a prayer meeting in hopes to get right with God and literally outside the doors of your prayer meeting there is an army massing with the intent to kill you? I bet we would pray our guts out in that moment because it literally could be our last.

As they were praying in desperation to the Lord, God answered.

> **Just as Samuel was sacrificing the burnt offering, the Philistines arrived to attack Israel. But the LORD spoke with a mighty voice of thunder from heaven that day, and the Philistines were thrown into such confusion that the Israelites defeated them. The men of Israel chased them from Mizpah to a place below Beth-car, slaughtering them all along the way. (1 Sam. 7:10-11 NLT)**

What an incredible intervention of the Lord! This would become a moment that would last in the hearts and minds of the people forever. They were about to die, but then God stepped in. The very next verse says, **"Samuel then took a large stone and placed it between the towns of Mizpah and Jeshanah. He named it Ebenezer (which means "the stone of help"), for he said, 'Up to this point the LORD has helped us!'" (1 Sam. 7:12 NLT).**

Samuel knew that they couldn't afford to forget what God was doing in that moment, and He raised a monument to ensure the people would remember how God had delivered them. Furthermore, he named it "Ebenezer." Remember, that was the name of the place where everything had previously turned for the worse. Ebenezer was the location Israel fought the Philistines over twenty years prior, and they were defeated, resulting in losing the ark of God. For 20+ years they had a bad taste in their mouth when the name Ebenezer was mentioned. But then, Samuel would redeem that name in the minds and hearts of the people. It would no longer be the name associated with their sin and loss of the presence of God represented by the ark. It would now be the name associated with God's

81

incredible, dramatic deliverance from the army that was ready to kill them.

We never like going through moments where we find ourselves at a prayer meeting with an army massing outside to kill us, because it forces us to have faith. Applying faith is not always easy and those situations are rarely comfortable. But if we can raise an Ebenezer in the moments God does break through with His power, we'll remember that moment the next time we face a trial. But, we have to remember. We have to celebrate what God has done in the past and what He is doing currently. What is God actively doing in your life in this moment in time? Is there something that you cannot afford to forget? Is there something He's already done in years past that you can bring to the forefront of your mind which will help you in the current trials you are facing?

When Nehemiah was rebuilding the wall and undergoing attacks from the enemy, he encouraged the people of Israel with these words: **Then as I looked over the situation, I called together the nobles and the rest of the people and said to them, "Don't be afraid of the enemy! Remember the Lord, who is great and glorious, and fight for your brothers, your sons, your daughters, your wives, and your homes!" (Neh. 4:14 NLT).**

His encouragement was to remember the Lord, Who is great and glorious! Remember why you're here. Remember why you're fighting. Remember Who you stand with. I think we can all receive that same encouragement to some degree.

Talk to somebody about what God is doing. We all tend to talk about things that interest us or things that we value. So, conversation about the things God is doing should be on our lips. If it's not, then perhaps we don't really value what God is doing all that much. We're not going to see Him do anything worth sharing if we're unwilling to share what He's already doing. He likes to be where He's celebrated.

If you have yet to put some systems in place that will help you to remember the things that the Lord is doing in your life, I want to encourage you to begin today. I currently use Evernote. It's a very handy filing system app you can download for free. I have notebooks in Evernote entitled dreams, healing testimonies, financial testimonies, stories to share, and dozens more. Whenever something happens that I don't want to forget, I log it. I refer back to these stories often to encourage myself and to build faith for the trials that lie ahead. I also have a chalkboard in my house where my wife creatively draws and or writes out major encounters I have had with the Lord. We hang that in our living room where I see it all the time. It is a constant reminder of the encounter I had with the Lord and keeps that Ebenezer before me all the time. Consider doing something similar so that a spirit of thankfulness and remembrance will continue to be in your life.

10
CONFESSION

One of the hardest things for me to do is to confess my sins to my wife. I imagine, if you are married, it might be much the same for you. She and I are accountability partners. We know everything about each other. All of our dirt, all of our struggles, all of our temptations, the things that have nothing to do with one another and those that are directly related to each other. I am discovering that the greatest amount of power is attached to the most difficult of honest confession. This may sound crazy but, often times confessing to God seems less impactful because there is not much "ouch" to that confession. I say this because I know He already knows my sins. He sees me inside and out. Now, don't get me wrong, I am certainly not saying that there is no power in confessing to the Lord. Scripture commands us to do so. Confession of sin to Him isn't to let Him know where we have fallen short, it's to invite Him into the healing process. Our confession to Him unshackles His wrists to heal and restore us.

Yahweh truly is omnipotent which means He's all powerful, but He has chosen to restrain Himself in certain capacities. Take for example, confession of sin. We first act in confessing and then He is enabled to respond to our first steps. Our confession allows Him to forgive our sin and to begin going to work against those sins on our behalf.

1 John 1:9 NLT says, **"But if we confess our sins to him, he is faithful and just to forgive us our sins and to cleanse us from all wickedness."**

If we confess…then He is faithful and just to forgive. That "if" rests on us. On the day I started writing this chapter, I had to confess something to my wife that was difficult to do. I knew it would hurt her, but in hurting her, I knew that it would also enable healing to come to the both of us. Still, I hate hurting her. When I do make mistakes, it is so difficult to confess them, though I know in my heart that embedded within my confession is an invitation to the Great Physician. It's an invitation that He will not deny.

I remember being at Sunday morning service in worship, wrestling within my mind on how to tell my wife my sin. I didn't want to, but I knew I had to. I had to commit before I could talk myself out of it so I texted her something very brief that incriminated me. Now there was no backing out. I knew I would have to further explain myself after I mentioned I messed up. Although obviously hurt, she was very understanding and forgiving.

It is difficult to confess, but it's even more difficult to be confessed to. She recognized my difficulty, and I also understood hers. Confession opens the door for both parties to dispense grace. It's both difficult to say and difficult to hear. If both parties are understanding what the other person is going through, there is a grace that comes upon both parties. If my wife would have lashed out at me immediately, chewed me up, spat me out only to chew me up again, it would destroy me. Even though that is what I deserved. I know I deserve to be lashed out against, chewed up, spat out and chewed up again, so her not doing so is dispensing a much-needed grace. Because I know she'll respond this way, it gives me strength to confess in the future. Please understand that this does not mean that we don't talk about it and it's not made abundantly clear the consequences of my sin. It's just done tactfully and with grace when emotions have subsided. This keeps her and I on the same team working against the devil together as husband and wife. It pulls each other out of the crosshairs and puts them appropriately on the devil. Not to excuse our collaboration with him which resulted in our sin but to refresh our minds on what is really happening behind the scenes.

Whenever something is confessed, it is brought to the light so that it can be exposed and then we can work on eradicating it completely. That usually means there are some adjustments that need to be made. It is not enough to confess our sins and never make any adjustments in order to keep us from sinning again in the future. When my wife and I talk about what's confessed, we often lay out a game plan for how we are going to make sure this doesn't happen again. What safeguards are we going to set in place to protect ourselves? The safeguards we set up are always reasonable considering the gravity of the situation. The sinner often downplays their sins and thinks them lesser than they actually are. So the accountability partner is likely the one who should ensure that beneficial, necessary safeguards are established.

A safeguard is a fence. But all through my childhood I hopped fences. It could be a fence with barbed wire on it. Well, I have even hopped over a few of those as well. It could be a fence with barbed wire, guard dogs, maybe a mine field, some sentry guns, and a wall of fire. But at the end of the day, it's still just a safeguard. Whether simple or extreme, safeguards do not make the root issue go away. They just make your determination all the more clear should you stumble in that area again. If you jump through several hoops and bypass multiple safeguards to indulge in your sin, you have a heart problem. It's not a mistake; it's a thought through trespass. Bottom line, decide what degree of safeguard is necessary for you. Know that this doesn't solve the problem, but it will help make the decisions to remain pure or fall again far clearer. Make the safeguards something that both parties agree on.

A green house is a man-made structure that creates an atmosphere conducive for the growth of certain plant life. Unconfessed sin is a spiritually built atmosphere conducive for the growth of sin. Sin is the spawn of darkness; darkness breeds more sin when kept in the dark. Shed some light on that darkness and the sin hiding there can't be kept in its cozy little abode any longer. The light of confession exposes what has been kept in the dark. Thus, confessed sin is a spiritually built atmosphere conducive for the overall righteous growth of the individual and the destruction of sin.

It is difficult for us to grasp how our sin hurts God. Sometimes we don't see ourselves like children hurting our Father, though we should. I confess that it is a difficult thing for me to do. However, when I see those who are my spiritual authority or those I am close to hurting because of my actions, it devastates me. I think God knew it would be difficult for us to have such understanding of the truth concerning how our sin hurts Him. So that is why He has commanded us not only to confess to Him, but also to one another.

"Confess your sins to each other and pray for each other so that you may be healed. The earnest prayer of a righteous person has great power and produces wonderful results" (James 5:16 NLT).

One of the most influential people in my life is my Tio. He is my dad's brother, and he mentored me when I was a teenager. God used him to be an incredible influence upon my life, and he still is to this day. When I was struggling with girls and gambling, he was working with me to overcome those struggles. I knew that every week we were going to meet up and he was going to ask me how I was doing in these areas. I loved that, and I hated that. I knew it was going to help me to change, but it was such a difficult thing to do. Sure I could lie to him, and believe me I did. But it didn't help that his wife, my Tia, is extremely prophetic and hears from God concerning me all the time. I kid you not, when I would sin during the week God would "tattle-tell" on me to her and then she would tell my Tio! I couldn't hide my sin in the dark even if I wanted to. They would pray and intercede for me and the Lord would show them Scriptures concerning me. As the Scriptures came forth they would get revelation from the Lord how they applied to me and then connect the dots. Obviously, they weren't looking for sins to pin on me, they were lifting me up before the Lord because they loved me. The Lord knew that what I needed most was correction. So he enabled those positioned in a place of honor within my life to bring that loving correction. When we would meet up for our discipleship meeting, he would ask me how I was doing with my struggles. If I lied, he would say, "What'd you do Thursday night at this time? Were you with so and so doing this and that?" The look of utter shock and awe mixed with the fear of the Lord would overwhelm my face, and there was no maintaining that lie any further. "YES I DID! I'M SORRY TIO!" Busted. God was going to make sure that my accountability was successful and that these sin issues were not going to be ignored. God clearly loves me enough to make sure I don't get away with things that will hurt me or others around me.

I can vividly remember stepping into a discipleship meeting with my Tio knowing that I had messed up during the week. When he asked me how I had been doing throughout the week, with my stomach in knots, I mustered up the courage to confess to him that yet again I had failed. He didn't get mad at me and tell me how dumb I was, or ask when I would finally get it right. Instead, he buried his face in his hands and wept bitterly right in front of me. I wish he would have just reprimanded me like I knew I deserved. I remember sitting there in that chair across from him at his desk as he cried and cried over my sin. This was the first time I had realized how my sins actually hurt someone. I felt like a dirt bag. I didn't know what to do in that moment but to sit there and take in all the pain I had caused. There was my Tio, pouring his life into mine. Praying for me regularly. Spending valuable time on my spiritual growth, and there appears to be such little growth in me. I was letting him down. I don't know if you have ever poured your life into someone only to see them fail time and time again; it's heart breaking.

After watching my Tio cry for several minutes, he very sternly looked at me and with tears still streaming down his face, told me to stop it. "Enough! Don't fall into those traps anymore."

With tears raining from my eyes I replied, "Yes sir." Then he walked around the table and embraced me. He held my head to his chest and kissed me several times telling me how much he loves me. He declared how much he believes in me and how much God has in store for my life, so that's why we have to overcome these struggles. He thanked me for confessing my sin to him and for being honest. This encounter has left such an impression on me that I think of it often and can recall the details as if it were yesterday.

Today I stand free from the two main struggles I faced while under my Tio's mentorship thanks to what he began and what others continued until complete freedom manifested. Praise God for that! The power of confession is a remarkable thing. You probably won't want to do it. Do it anyways. Make sure you have somebody in your life that you trust enough to be vulnerable with but make sure this is a person that will keep you accountable. Don't find accountability that frowns at our sin and nothing more. Find someone who truly cares about your spiritual condition and will lovingly do what it takes to ensure you walk in freedom. Confessing invites the Great Physician to come and heal, an invitation He will not ignore.

11
Don't Get Stuck

When I was learning to spend considerable amounts of time in prayer, there was a specific way I liked the room. I would typically pray in a dark room with loud music. I liked some space so that I could walk around because I pace when I pray. That was my default setting while spending time with the Lord, and it was effective. I felt like I connected well with the Lord in that setting and had wonderful times of prayer and worship. One day His presence never manifested, and I felt like I didn't connect well with Him at all. Was there sin in my life? Was I distracted? Was I just not feeling it? Nothing seemed to make sense because all my questions checked out okay. I wrote it off as a fluke, and the next time I went to pray, I set up my default prayer atmosphere and started pressing in again. Nothing. It felt dry as a bone once again. What's wrong with me? What am I doing wrong? Whenever I do this, He shows up, and now He's not.

I remembered a preacher who was praying for people to get filled with the Holy Spirit encourage the audience to not get stuck, to keep crying out until the breakthrough came. I felt that perhaps I was getting stuck, and I didn't like that. I wasn't sure what to do. I knew I was wholeheartedly attempting to engage with my Father in prayer and worshipping Him with a pure heart, but there was seemingly no response from Him. I have to admit that was frustrating. Then while praying after weeks of this bothersome issue I had the random idea pop into my head to go on a walk and pray. This was entirely different than my default dark-room, loud-music time alone with the Lord; however, that apparently wasn't working so by this point I was desperate for a touch from God. I started walking down this beautiful horse trail behind our church and wouldn't you know it, the presence of the Lord came rushing back onto me. At times, I would stop on the sidewalk of a busy road and weep because the presence of the Lord was so strong.

I was determined to do whatever it took to engage with God. I was determined to go wherever His presence was. My "formula" for prayer with Him was changing and I had to be determined enough not to get stuck in the ways I had always done things. Religion keeps us doing the same thing over and over because we're told it's a good thing. But Isaiah prophesied, **"For I am about to do something new. See, I have already begun! Do you not see it?" (Isa. 43:19 NLT).**

God is doing something new, and we cannot afford to rely on the way we have always done things and expect that to bring forth the fruit it's always brought forth. We have to remain flexible. We have to follow what the Spirit is doing. He is unchanging, but the way He does things is often fresh. We have to remain current with what the Holy Spirit is saying and doing in order to determine what has His fingerprints on it. If God is breathing on hymns and not on our modern day contemporary music, then I will sing those hymns with everything in me. If the wind of the Spirit is blowing on a particular dance, location, lighting, or act of service then that's what I want to be doing. I know that God looks at the heart and in some respect these things don't matter much. It's how we connect with God that matters most and I would agree.

Spending quality time connecting with my wife is simply different when we're paintballing together as to when we're having a romantic dinner on the beach. Are we still connecting in both activities? Yes, but it's much different. She gets far more excited and responds more to my pursuit of her with dinner on a beach than crawling through the dirt being shot at on the paintball field. I can't imagine why. As you would imagine, our pursuit of the Lord is much the same.

As you may have guessed, it wasn't very long before the presence of the Lord lifted from my prayer walks. This time I knew better than to let weeks pass by in frustration. I began to seek the Lord on what He wanted me to do next. Consistent with the nature of God, He would choose something even more uncomfortable and sacrificial than before. He was now asking me to wake up before the sun would rise and spend time with Him in prayer in worship. For me, this was a big deal. I sure do love my sleep, and I'm always up pretty late. It's as if God was asking me, "How far are you willing to go to get Me?" He was testing me to see when I would get stuck. So for the next several months, it meant being up super early praying in the morning on the living room floor while everybody else was sleeping. Many times falling asleep in prayer which I justified by saying, "God can't give me dreams if I don't fall asleep, sooooooo…" I confess that this wasn't my favorite time to pray, but I could feel the pleasure of the Lord enveloping my life through my passion to discover Him again and again.

Then another shift came and I found myself back in a prayer room but this time not to walk around like I had always done. Now He sat me down and settled me from moving at all, but just to think on Him. Seasons came where I didn't pray much of anything but just listened to Him. Other seasons of solely worship, and others of solely praying in the Spirit. Whatever I felt Him leading me to do, that's what I was determined to do so that I wouldn't get stuck. I still practice this today.

As of recently God has been using the middle of the night cries of my kids as my spiritual alarm clock to pray.

93

When my son Judah starts crying, I fall out of bed and walk throughout the house putting him back to sleep while engaging with God in prayer and worship. I admit, this is the hardest season I've been in. However, I must say that I don't ever feel like God is judging my performance with each time of prayer with Him. He's not setting the timer for how many minutes I spend with Him in the middle of the night. He's not looking for an opportunity to accuse me of slipping. He sees my heart from a broader perspective, and I know He is pleased with me. When I really focus in on Him and spend good quality time with my Father, I know that He smiles upon me. When I fail and barely fix my mind on Him while rocking my kids back to sleep and then doze off, I don't feel as if He is mad at me. I think I am harder on myself in those situations than He is on me. That doesn't give me permission to be lazy, but it does say a lot about my Father in Heaven. He is a good Daddy Who is pleased with us when we make the effort. My son is learning how to high five right now. When he doesn't get it right, or when he misses my hand, I don't reprimand him or punish him. He is trying and he is learning; so am I when I give my Father "high fives" in the place of prayer.

James 4:8 NKJV gives us an incredible key to encountering God, and it was mentioned earlier, **"Draw near to God and He will draw near to you."**

We are the ones who initiate the encounter with Him by our first drawing near to God. That faith in moving towards Him, He responds to. I remember when we had our typical Wednesday night youth service and I was determined to get a touch from God. I wasn't feeling His presence all day and honestly was feeling pretty dry all around. While worship was going on, I told God, "I'm not getting off this floor until You touch me!" I was pretty desperate. The worship set ended and I could sense that everybody was waiting on me, the pastor, to transition us out of worship and onto the rest of the service like I do every other week, but I wasn't moving. In fact, all I did was crawl from the front middle of the room to the side of the room where I wouldn't be too much of a distraction as I continued to press into God for His touch. I can't give what I don't have and I'd rather not minister void of all anointing if at all possible. One of my leaders took over the service and preached a message instead of me (we were prepared for moments like this) and after a couple hours when everybody had left the building, somebody came and whispered in my ear that everybody had left and they were leaving too. I still didn't have my touch from God. Finally it was quiet and dark in the room, and I thought to myself that this certainly was going to be the moment the touch was going to come. I waited and waited and prayed and prayed and still nothing. It was getting very late, my wife was at home probably wondering where in the world I was; I was hungry, tired and starting to get a little frustrated to be honest.

I finally decided to get up off the floor and go home, eat a little soup and then try again in my living room. I said once again, "Okay, I'm not getting off THIS floor until You touch me." Well guess what...I fell asleep on that carpet that night and never received any touch from Him.

When morning came, my first thought was disappointment. But then it was followed by another thought. I didn't receive the touch from God that night, but I believe I received something even better, the *pursuit* of the touch. If God would have blasted me like I was hoping He would, it would have been a cool story of how I pressed in until the breakthrough came, a lesson I'd already learned several times over. Instead, this time I learned how to continue to engage with God for days, weeks, months, even years on end in order to receive from Him whatever it is He's desiring to get to me.

The great things He has for us don't come cheap. Learning to not get stuck while believing for family members to get saved, miracles to manifest, relationships to heal, revival to sweep the city is a wildly valuable life-long lesson worth learning. My encouragement to you is: don't get stuck. Whatever it is your crying out for, if you know that it is God's will, don't give up on that. In addition to that persevering faith, don't get stuck in the same way of doing things. Allow Him to guide you. His guidance is not always a shove in a specific direction, it's often a gentle nudge one way or another. Something we can easily miss if we are not looking for it. Whatever comes to your mind that you think might be the Lord, try it out. Change up your music, time of prayer or worship, location, activity, alone, with a partner, working out, shower, dark, light, in English, in the Spirit, loud, quiet...ANYTHING that comes to mind.

It's silly to continue doing something that's not working and labeling it faithful. Fruitless faithfulness is a favorite trap of the enemy. If the way you're connecting with God is simply not working, it may be because you're stuck in a rut and He's trying to get you to find Him again. The Lord loves playing hide and seek. It's not that what you've always done is a bad thing. It just might not be the best thing for this season in your life that the Lord is bringing you into. So don't get frustrated that it's not working. Instead, get excited that there's a new adventure you're about to embark on. An adventure that will take you to new places in the wonderful presence of Almighty God if you resolve not to get stuck.

12
FALLING IN LOVE

Perhaps one of the most difficult challenges of my life has been to remain so passionately in love with Jesus that every day is like the first day of our honeymoon. Now, I know that I love Him and He has all my heart, but I confess that I certainly don't treat every day like it is the first day of our honeymoon.

That first day of the honeymoon right after getting married is an extremely special day. I remember waking up in La Jolla, CA right across from the beach and the first thing I saw was my new bride's beautiful face. Of course, the day we were married was particularly special, but I like to emphasize the first day of the honeymoon because it is the first full day together as husband and wife. The day is filled with romance, joy, laughs, fun, consideration, surprises, memories, and so many other wonderful things. What a special day. There is a lot of grace dispensed towards each other on that day. It is almost as if your spouse could do no wrong, and the both of you are determined to make the day as enjoyable as possible.

What if we adopted this mindset and took it to our relationship with the greatest Lover of all? What if we treated Him like He really was a big deal? What if we woke up each day eager to romance God and be romanced by Him? To partake of His joy, laugh together, have some fun out and about our day. What if we were considerate enough to care what He thought concerning all that happened within our day? What if He surprised us all throughout the day and we showed Him how much we loved it? What if we built memories with God together each and every day? Precious moments that we couldn't forget even if we tried. What if we fell in love with God every single day? This, dear friends, is the adventure of a lifetime I choose to joyfully embrace.

If somebody were to ask me if I loved God, my response would obviously be yes. I have loved Him for as long as I can remember. If somebody were to ask me if I fell in love with God today…I'm not so sure my answer would be yes. Perhaps many of us are still riding the "in love with God" wave generated some years or even decades ago. I'm not saying that is a bad thing, but what I would like to propose to you is that we might be missing the tsunami-like love beckoning us today. I could surely tell my wife I love her because I married her on August 20th, 2010 and it would be true. But instead, I'm challenged to fall deeper in love with her today, tomorrow, and the next day.

In 2004, the movie *50 First Dates* was released. Drew Barrymore's character relives the same day over and over again because she suffers from short-term memory loss due to a car accident. Those in her family and daily routine are all in on a set up to keep her unsuspicious to the fact that it's not actually the day she thinks it is. All is going well till she meets Adam Sandler's character who falls in love with her at first sight. His challenge is to get her to fall in love with him, and if he's successful, he'll have to do it again the next day. I'm reminded of a line in the movie where Drew Barrymore's character says, "I was so nervous to come here and meet the guy who makes me fall in love with him every day." Adam's character was so head over heels in love with Barrymore's that he would win her heart every single day no matter what. I'm convinced, God wants us to take Him on 50 first dates. Unlike Adam Sandler's character, we don't have to convince God to fall in love with us, but we do get to pursue Him daily with a confidence that we will surely win His heart if we make this pursuit a priority.

It makes perfect sense why I would love a King like Jesus, but it doesn't make much sense at all to see why He would love me back. Pastor Bill Johnson says, "Everybody wants a King like Jesus." It's true. He's perfect in every way! I, on the other hand, am imperfect in every way. I've broken His heart time and time again. Spat in His face, laughed about it, and repeated it all over again. We are a bunch of walking messes.

So why would this perfect King love us so much? How is it that He desires to pursue us? This is quite possibly the most unfathomable reality of the world. If you will let it sink in, it will rock your world. His power, beauty, strength, authority, might, glory, and ridiculous love is chasing after me. My frailty, rebellion, wickedness, pride, selfishness, hatred, lust, and sinful-self is not worth being chased. Yet, still He does. Unbelievable.

At the beginning of John chapter 13, Jesus does something crazy:

> **Before the Passover celebration, Jesus knew that his hour had come to leave this world and return to his Father. He had loved his disciples during his ministry on earth, and now he loved them to the very end. It was time for supper, and the devil had already prompted Judas, son of Simon Iscariot, to betray Jesus. Jesus knew that the Father had given him authority over everything and that he had come from God and would return to God. So he got up from the table, took off his robe, wrapped a towel around his waist, and poured water into a basin. Then he began to wash the disciples' feet, drying**

them with the towel he had around him. (John 13:1-5 NLT)

This is crazy to me because Jesus is near the end of His life, and He knows that He is going to be betrayed by one of His closest friends. He already knows that it's Judas that's going to betray Him, and what does He do? He washes Judas' feet. He serves Judas. What an incredible picture of how we certainly do not deserve His love by any stretch of the imagination yet He takes it upon Himself to serve us. To love us. I say again, unfathomable.

God commanded the fire on the altar in the temple never to go out. The priests were commissioned to tend the flame on the altar in order to keep it burning. Only through the constant attention that fire received from the priests was it able to keep burning. If it was neglected in any way, the fuel (wood) would be consumed and the fire would burn itself out. Constant fuel had to be added and the fire tended.

What a beautiful analogy for the fire of His love for us and our love for Him being forever tended. His love will never diminish for us, but our love will certainly burn out for Him if we don't continually add fuel to the fire and stoke the flame. This is ultimately the purpose behind why I wrote this book and entitled it *Fuel the Fire*. I pray that whoever reads this will be stashing kindling and chopping firewood for their own personal flames of intimacy with the King. I pray this will help them fall in love with Him again and again, every single day of their lives.

I'm sure you have seen those electric, fake fireplaces. They digitally project flames and give off heat. The whole thing is fake looking and simply plugs in for a continual manufactured fire. This fire never burns out…or does it? Technically this fire never really gets started. It is a counterfeit of the real thing. Sounds like a type of Christian

I'm all too familiar with. Sounds pretty similar to the types of churches that don't want to get their hands dirty by chopping firewood, stashing kindling, striking a match, and tending the flame to ensure it keeps burning. They would prefer to just flip the switch when they show up at church on Sunday morning and display fake flames, that give off a little bit of heat but never really consume anything.

Worst of all, there's no maintenance necessary to the flame. You fell in love with God a long time ago so you got plugged into the power source and now you just ride that wave until the day you die. There is no need to keep fresh fuel on the fire in order to steward the flame and ensure you are falling in love with Almighty God every single day. Once was enough. Perhaps it's true that falling in love with Him once long ago was enough to get you into Heaven, but it's not enough to get Heaven on earth. Furthermore, the incredible love encounters with Him that are awaiting us on earth will certainly never happen. It may be convenient to flip the switch, but that is not what I signed up for. I get bored looking at those fake fire places, but I never get bored of watching a real flame burn.

A real fire can be started anywhere. These fake fire places have to be plugged in. When you're accustomed to the fake, flip-the-switch Christianity, you'll never find yourself venturing very far from an outlet. You'll always want to make sure you can flip the switch at any given time and your relationship with God will be good. God forbid the power ever goes out and your counterfeit relationship with God will be exposed. Those whose flames burn with authenticity daringly go where they feel the Spirit of God lead because their relationships with the Lord are mobile. They can burn anywhere. They don't need their devotional book, music playlist, Sunday morning sermon or even small group. All of those things are great and I use them too, but I do not rely on them to burn for the things of God. They are certainly beneficial to growing faith but all we truly need is Him. If all those tools disappeared what would happen to our faith? What if we lost every encouraging tool to our walk with God? What if we didn't have access to a Bible? Is our relationship with God sustainable enough that it wouldn't matter? I'd venture to say it might even get stronger. Some of my most precious moments with the Lord were when I had no cell-service, Bible in hand, or any other wonderful tool. Just Him. Here's what I'm trying to say: when fires are fueled, they grow. So should our faith in God. Even if His breath is all that fans our flames.

I would never advocate for removing those great tools I just mentioned when your partnership with them is healthy. However, I would caution those who's dependability on those things replaces their dependance upon the Lord which is unhealthy. They are to be an enhancement not a replacement. Pastor Brian Ross once preached, "You will find that your greatest fulfillment is when your walk with God intersects with your relationships with others." Having just one or the other is not the fullest picture. The greater my relationship with God becomes, the more it ought it to intersect and overflow into my relationships all around me. Use these tools to strengthen your walk with God, so that it's so healthy you no longer rely on them for growth. They are a beautiful enhancement to your already thriving faith. Then overflow your walk with God unto the lives all around you. Let the tools assist in building an even more solid faith in God.

When John is asked to write a letter to the angel of the church of Ephesus, he pens:

This is the message from the one who holds the seven stars in his right hand, the

one who walks among the seven gold lampstands:
"I know all the things you do. I have seen your hard work and your patient endurance. I know you don't tolerate evil people. You have examined the claims of those who say they are apostles but are not. You have discovered they are liars. You have patiently suffered for me without quitting.
"But I have this complaint against you. You don't love me or each other as you did at first! (Rev. 2:1-4 NLT)

They are getting praised for all that they have been doing right but there was this one thing against them. They had lost their first love. Not that they didn't love anymore at all, but that they didn't love like they did at the beginning. It is a picture of the individual who falls in love and attempts to ride that same wave for the rest of their lives without choosing to fall in love again and again and again! We could be doing a lot of things right, but there is still a bone He has to pick with us if we are not continually falling head over heels in love with Him every day. He daily chooses to give Himself to us, why would He not expect the same from us in return?

In September of 2017, our young adult ministry hosted our first annual conference called "Love Conference." I knew the name would potentially throw people off and they might think it was a marriage conference of some sort but I couldn't shake the name. I had lots of other names that would have fit as well, but keeping it all about falling in love with Him was all that really mattered to me. "Falling In Love Again" was the main theme for the conference. Every shirt, hoodie, lanyard or cup was reminding its owner to fall in love with Almighty God that day. I've heard many testimonies since that conference that these reminders have been effective.

I was raised Christian and have a truly remarkable spiritual heritage. My dad is still a licensed minister, evangelist, and writer. My mom absolutely loves God and carries incredible wisdom and moves in gifts of the Spirit. I have aunts and uncles who have been in full time ministry for many years and carry a spiritual maturity that commands attention. I had every opportunity to be ridiculously successful. Still, in my late teens I chose to do the things I wanted to do. I was chasing girls, blowing money at casinos, disrespecting the rules of my house and living very self-indulged. All the while I was still going to church every Sunday and youth group every Wednesday. I was becoming quite lukewarm.

My cousin, who was the youth pastor at the time, wanted to take our youth group and leadership team to a Jesus Culture conference. One of the first ones actually. The conference was held at Bethel church in Redding, California, and we drove about 12 hours to get there. When we arrived, we were a little bit late and had to sit in an overflow room to watch the conference on screen. *This is ridiculous*, I thought to myself. *We drove all this way and now we get stuck in this overflow room...ugh!* I had my little pity party for a few minutes but then composed myself and decided I wasn't going to let this hinder my desire to reconnect with God over the weekend. As the worship team began to start their first song, I slipped out of my seat and found a place on the carpet in the back of the room by myself where I could engage with God.

Just when I got there, the back doors to the overflow room swung open and in came rushing all of the Bethel School of Supernatural Ministry students. They came flooding into the room dancing and shouting their way into worship. The whole room was taken aback at first; I know I was. I watched for a few minutes as grown men unashamedly danced ballet in the back of the room. Others jumped, shouted, cried, and danced as if nobody was watching them. These interns and students were around my age or maybe a little older and I was seeing a passion in them that I knew was somewhere deep in me. Something about what they carried was prophesying to me. Their undignified worship was giving me permission to rise to the occasion and be who God had been calling me to be my whole life.

After the amazing conference ended and we were driving back home to San Diego from Northern California, I could remember staring out the window at the farm rows and thinking to myself how things were going to be different from this point forward. I was going to live how God had called me to live, and I wasn't going to turn back. I had fallen in love with Jesus afresh and anew. That moment had marked me, and I now tell it as the turning point of my life.

When I came home, I had such a hunger to pray and worship. I couldn't wait until evening came when I would play some loud worship music in my dark, small bedroom and I would sing and dance until I was exhausted. This happened night after night. I knew my dad had to go to work early in the morning and his bedroom was right next to mine but I couldn't help myself. I was in love.

My dad never once complained by the way. I think he knew that his son falling in love with God was more important than a good night's sleep. It was in that bedroom that I learned to fall in love with God day after day. Weeping on that carpet. Dancing like a goofball all around the room. Interceding for anybody and everybody that came to mind. I remember lifting my hands and feeling like there were thousands of angels behind me worshipping Yahweh with me; I could almost feel them. There was a fire burning inside of me. There was a passion stirring within me. There was a Lover I was getting to know on a scale I'd never ventured into before. I was falling in love, day after day after day.

This is my story. What's yours? I hope that you are challenged to forever endeavor the most satisfying adventure anybody could ever experience—falling in love with the greatest Lover of all, every single day of our lives.

It's always been about love, from the very beginning,
And it will always be about love, till the very ending.
-Jake Hamilton

13

SUPERNATURAL

Everything God does is supernatural because He is a supernatural being. I have noticed that as I have gotten older there has been a subtle shift from believing in a supernatural God to diminishing my faith to believing in only that of a practical God. Far too many people have convinced themselves that God has given us "common sense." If it is common, there is a good chance it didn't come from God. There is not much common sense in a 100-year-old Abraham conceiving a child and fathering a nation. There is not much common sense in Noah building an ark on dry land because a flood is coming when the earth had never even experienced rain. There is not much common sense in sending Joseph to prison in order to get him to the palace. There is not much common sense in heading toward a sea with a newly freed nation without any boats in hope to escape the strongest army on the face of the planet. There is not much common sense in sending a boy to fight a giant. There is not much common sense in putting worshippers in front of soldiers and sending them into battle. There is not much common sense in taking sinners and uneducated men and using them to change the world and build the church upon. There is not much common sense in a perfect supernatural God coming to die for a world that He loves but for the most part does not love Him back. If we reduce the activity of God to that of common sense, I fear we're missing God altogether.

Emma, my 2-and-a-half-year-old daughter at the time of my writing this sometimes gets scared and when she tells us, our response is simply, "You don't have anything to be scared of because you have Jesus." After hearing this over and over again, her response begins to change in scary situations where she even now sometimes tells others, "Don't be scared; you have Jesus." She doesn't know that He is the God of the angel armies, and that He has victory over the principalities and powers of this world; His triumphant work of Calvary has made a spectacle of the devil's defeat, and He forever reigns on the throne over all the universe! All she knows is, because of Jesus, she's not scared anymore.

It is very simple. I think Jesus knew that men would begin to forget about a supernatural God and think only in practicalities and that's why He made such a strong point to be like children. Matthew 19:13-14 NLT says:

> **One day some parents brought their children to Jesus so he could lay his hands on them and pray for them. But the disciples scolded the parents for bothering him.**
> **But Jesus said, "Let the children come to me. Don't stop them! For the Kingdom of Heaven belongs to those who are like these children."**

"The Kingdom of Heaven belongs to those who are like these children." Children have this simple and supernatural faith. I love preaching to kids because in many ways they haven't rationalized their faith and tainted their belief in a supernatural God. It's still fresh. They still believe in the God of the impossible. It's not a watered-down religion. They are open to pray for the supernatural power of God to intervene in their lives. To them, the possibilities of God's power are endless. I remember seeing a video of a young boy testifying to God's healing power at a stadium crusade and while being interviewed he simply said, "I believe Jesus can do anything." What a beautiful perspective! It doesn't matter what it is, Jesus can do anything.

Ephesians 3:20 NLT states, **"Now all glory to God, who is able, through his mighty power at work within us, to accomplish infinitely more than we might ask or think."** If we can think it, He can accomplish infinitely more than that. I don't know about you but I can imagine quite a bit…He can do more. He is a supernatural God.

But in order for God to do that supernatural thing that is so great, we have to understand that it might not be practical. Which means we won't be able to plan it out in ten steps. We won't be able to schedule it. We won't be able to compile it into a pretty packaged business plan. I am not saying that all of those things are bad, but I am saying that those are very practical ideas—they are saturated in common sense. I've tried many of them. I've gone to several conferences on healing and every formula has failed. I've read many books on the subject and once again acquired only disappointment. Am I doing something wrong? I'm reading with an open heart and a genuine desire to help other people, aren't I? Does God see something in me that I don't currently see? Perhaps there's not a formula to this. I'm discovering that there are Kingdom truths that absolutely apply and they give glimpses to the nature of God which helps me know how to pray and believe. However, at the end of the day it would appear that God has covered His tracks well enough that we as humans can't do what we always do, which is build this into a formula. A formula that can be marketed and sold for quite a profit.

Let's take a look at one of the most remarkable stories in all of Scripture:

> **One day Moses was tending the flock of his father-in-law, Jethro, the priest of Midian. He led the flock far into the**

109

wilderness and came to Sinai, the mountain of God. There the angel of the LORD appeared to him in a blazing fire from the middle of a bush. Moses stared in amazement. Though the bush was engulfed in flames, it didn't burn up. "This is amazing," Moses said to himself. "Why isn't that bush burning up? I must go see it."

When the LORD saw Moses coming to take a closer look, God called to him from the middle of the bush, "Moses! Moses!" "Here I am!" Moses replied. (Ex. 3:1-4 NLT)

Notice that it was when Moses was coming in to take a closer look that God called to him from the burning bush. It wasn't when Moses was passing by with the sheep. It wasn't when Moses first noticed the burning bush. It was when he drew himself closer to investigate in awe this supernatural manifestation.

I believe there are burning bush moments all around us every single day. There are moments of supernatural manifestation at our workplaces, schools, churches, grocery stores, and if we would stir up our faith to believe that our God still moves supernaturally, we would begin to take notice of these burning bushes. Not only would we notice these burning bushes everywhere, but I believe that we would also begin to hear the voice of the Lord calling out to us from the midst of that supernatural moment. I wonder what God is saying to me today? I may never know if I don't draw myself into the supernatural burning bushes all around me.

What if God's voice to you today isn't found in your daily devotion? What if it is not found in your daily Bible reading plan? What if it is not found in the sermon you are listening to or your favorite song you're singing along with while you drive? What if the voice of God speaking to you today is found in a burning bush supernatural encounter that you have with somebody at the bank? What if it is found in a conversation with a stranger at a gas station? What if it's in the second to last point your pastor preaches this upcoming Sunday? What if your burning bush moment takes place on your commute home from work? I'm certainly not advocating for discarding our devotionals, podcasts, worship music, or anything else we use to draw into the presence of the Lord, but I am advocating for opening our eyes to see the supernatural manifestations all around us because we may just find God in those encounters. When we give value to the supernatural activity of God all around us, it boosts our faith. When our faith rises, the activity of God increases. The cycle goes round and round as the world gets impacted through our partnership with God.

But what if you don't feel Him doing much? In one of Jake Hamilton's songs he sings, "Your presence muted, teaches me to have faith." You may not be able to feel Him doing what you're doing, but have faith. He always responds to faith. Rest assured, even if you don't feel Him near, you know that He is.

If we were to just glance at these burning bushes and pass them by because we simply don't care or believe in that sort of thing, then there may be a nation in need of deliverance that will remain in captivity; that was Moses' case. Maybe some of us are too busy tending our sheep, getting good grades, building our family, chasing our career, enjoying our hobbies, and consequently we're missing the burning bushes all around us. Yes, do all of the above, but without compromising our necessity for the supernatural. How much is riding not only on our

111

acceptance but our pursuit of the supernatural power of God? A nation? A state? A city? A school? A church? A small group? A friend?

The text continues, **"'Do not come any closer,' the LORD warned. 'Take off your sandals, for you are standing on holy ground.'"** The ground wasn't holy a moment ago. But now that God is present, everything becomes holy in that degree of His presence. We read Exodus 29:43 NLT in an earlier chapter but it fits well here also, **"I will meet the people of Israel there, in the place made holy by My glorious presence."** So getting into His presence is more than just goosebumps and the hair standing up on the back of our necks; it's about becoming holy. Worship is always the appropriate response to holiness. It's why angels are constantly encircling the throne of God crying out, "HOLY, HOLY, HOLY!" The revelation of His holiness merits a response of true worship.

"'I am the God of your father—the God of Abraham, the God of Isaac, and the God of Jacob.' When Moses heard this, he covered his face because he was afraid to look at God" (Ex. 3:6 NLT). God was introducing Himself to Moses and Moses was freaked out. He covered his face because he was afraid to look at God. If we were to fast forward the story, we would discover that Moses' relationship didn't stay this way. He would later tell Yahweh in Exodus 33:18 NKJV, **"Please, Show me Your glory!"** He'd walked with Him enough to fall in love with Him. To respect God. To be close to Him. Worship is intimacy. Intimacy is reserved for lovers. At their meeting, Moses couldn't look at Him; later in life, Moses couldn't keep his eyes off Him. In fact, right after Moses cries out to God to show him His glory, God tells Moses that He will hide Moses in a crevice of a rock and cover him with His hand as He walks by. Why did He have to cover Moses with

His hand as He walked by? I believe that Moses was so overwhelmingly in love with God, and so desperately wanting to see His glory that He didn't care if he died looking at Him in that moment. He just wanted to see Him. I believe Yahweh knew that and covered him with His hand so he wouldn't die. Moses couldn't keep his eyes off Him. Sounds like love to me.

Some more fascinating things happen in this story but I want to capitalize on this main thing. Moses was not the practical, common sense choice for the job. He wasn't a leader, he stuttered, he'd killed a man…the deck was stacked against him. But one thing he had going for him was his appreciation for the supernatural. Perhaps one of the most gnarly supernatural manifestations of God's power was going to be displayed through Moses' obedience, so God chose a man who was hungry for the supernatural. When he saw a burning bush, he drew in closer to get a better look. This was where his belief in the God of the impossible began.

Charles Swindoll once said, "The impossible is God's ideal." I want to encourage you to seek this supernatural God. I want to highlight the difference between *accepting* God doing supernatural things in your midst and *seeking after* God doing supernatural things in your midst. Unfortunately, some have so wanted not to be weird that we've swung the pendulum in the opposite direction too far. Fear has set into the hearts of believers who are scared to fall into weirdness or don't see the value in the supernatural. Newsflash, every Biblical supernatural occurrence is weird. Some people, on the other hand, tend to only seek the supernatural things of God. They care more for what He can do than for who He is. No good relationship comes from that. But it's equally ignorant to assume that His activity will always fit within the confines of what we'll allow, not what He wants to do. Something practical and full of sense. Well, according to Scripture, I don't see a whole lot of that either. I've seen leaders on both sides of the fence argue their position till they're blue in the face. This isn't helping anybody, and it only shows the world a divided Christian front. I think we should land appropriately in the middle. Inviting God to come, however He wants to do so. If the ball is in His court to come do as He pleases, nobody should get upset as to how He chooses to come. Unless of course they'd rather be God instead of Him. I simply want Him to display His love in power and saving grace no matter what. Ask the Holy Spirit to help transform our mindset back to that of a child. Let's not be bogged down with the practicalities of life in all of their common sense. We ought to remain humble without thinking that we have matured beyond believing in the supernatural. His heart for us is quite the opposite. To hunger for the Kingdom supernatural is to hunger for God Himself.

Something within us is crying out for the supernatural. The "more" that this world cannot offer. I believe it's why Hollywood has such success in movies on the paranormal, supernatural, and superhero genres. So many people are done with the plain old practical world we live in. When they can escape for a couple hours and watch The Avengers battle evil and protect our world for the good of humanity, something inside of us relates to them. Perhaps we aren't billionaires with Iron Man suits, or a super old, extremely fit, righteous Captain America, or a temper riddled Hulk, but our innate desire for good, coupled with a realization of the supernatural, renders us more similar to superheroes than we think.

When we read the stories of the Bible, we ought to see them as permissions being granted to us. If it is true that we will see things that eye has not seen, hear things that ear has not heard, and do things never before done, then we should look at our lives and ask ourselves, are we even seeing a glimpse of the things we read about in Scripture? Jesus' famous words, "Greater things you will do" both excite me and haunt me. I want to do those greater things, but I'm not! Something has to change. When Jesus goes up on the mountaintop to pray and He's transfigured, we should expect some similar supernatural encounters when we go to God in prayer. Has it ever happened to me? Nope. Am I spending every day asking for it to happen? Nope. However, am I making it clear that God can come and do whatever He pleases as I seek Him in the place of prayer…ABSOLUTELY! Do I think God is offended if I begin to ask Him for those types of encounters, absolutely not! I think He gets excited just like He did when Jonathan and his armor bearer took on the Philistines. Or when the newly persecuted Church prayed for boldness to keep preaching the Gospel even though they were getting beaten for it and the earth shook underneath them.

 We cannot expect in faith for God to encounter us, but then place parameters on how He can respond. We forget that He alone is sovereign; we are not. He can do whatever He wants! We place all this red tape around our prayers and yet we wonder why God doesn't seem to answer like we thought He would. We throw the baby out with the bath water and discard everything supernatural because it's either apparently not working or we rationalize away our circumstances. Then to make matters worse, we create demonic induced doctrines that make us feel better about the fact that we don't see anything supernatural in our lives whatsoever. Our practical, rationalized thinking somehow takes the clearly supernatural happenings found all throughout the Bible and the invitation to follow suit and either ignores it or wages war against it. Some of us ought to be careful. The evidence of what God is doing in the earth is often supernatural and many have labeled it the works of the devil. Pastor Bill Johnson says, "It's blasphemy to attribute to God the very work of the devil." Be careful to not call what God is doing the actions of the devil.

Funny, people get more upset about this type of topic than perhaps any other I've discovered. What is there to fight about? The power of God doing what we clearly see in the Bible? Why is that bad? I honestly believe that the devil is so terrified of a Church filled with power that He's gone to extreme lengths to keep the Church at large, powerless. He's not afraid of a powerless Church. He's fine with us drinking coffee, eating donuts, hanging more lights, and singing more songs even if we all go to Heaven. But He's terrified of us moving in power. The promise of the Baptism in the Holy Spirit was power from on high, not just tongues. I would even dare to say that the enemy would be happy with us praying in tongues as long as we never move in genuine power. It's no wonder why Christians are fighting themselves over the topic of power for as long as I can remember.

Subtly, the enemy has crept in and crippled the Church from moving in power. We see a small dosage of power in a healing or miracle every so often. Just enough to keep our theology intact, but we never step into the power He paid for us to walk in. The same power that raised Christ Jesus from the dead. Instead of crying out for God to break this off of us and release His power in mighty ways so that the world will know and believe that He is Lord, we keep each other in the crosshairs, stiffen up our upper lips, sneering at one another as we hold to our position. Foolish. We need to repent. We need to come before God broken, and through faith, invite His power back into our lives. In particular, the American Church. I know some places move

116

in power right now, and it's amazing. Guess what? They are by no means perfect. Neither is my church, nor yours. Nevertheless, they are not the standard. Jesus alone is our standard. We should be striving for all that He says we can have and we should be praying to do all that He says we can do. PERIOD.

If you have settled for a life void of the supernatural, my heart breaks for you. I am not currently seeing the manifestation of the supernatural at the degree that I am yearning for, but I am certainly not giving that up. I am promoting the pursuit of a supernatural God who can do whatever He wants in my life, even if it is uncomfortable in the eyes of the world. Biblical Christianity looks like a supernatural lifestyle. Don't settle. Don't lower the standard of Scripture. Don't lower the standard modeled through Jesus' life. Be encouraged to seek after this. Put effort and faith into welcoming the supernatural power of God into your life. Restore that childlike faith and introduce the supernatural power of God into your day-to-day lifestyle.

14
JIREH

Whenever God reveals Himself in our life in any way, a facet of His character is demonstrated to us. When He heals, His character as the Healer is made known. When He neutralizes a tumultuous situation, His character as Peace is made known. When He doesn't change Who He is, He is unchanging. There are several names of God found all throughout Scripture that are all revealing different parts of His character, but there is one name that I've come to know perhaps better than the rest: Jehovah Jireh - The Lord my Provider. God's provision is certainly not limited to money. He is also El Roi, meaning the God Who sees, and you can rest assured that He sees your situation and knows what you have need of. He knows how to meet that need according to His riches in glory in Christ Jesus. Oftentimes our need is not more money; it is something we don't even know how to ask for. This is where we have to learn to trust that He knows us better than we know ourselves and sees our situation from a perspective we simply do not have. Learning to pray for His will to be done in our lives and for His provision to accompany His will is wisdom.

He is a good Father. A good Father knows how to take care of His kids. His kids learn to trust Him because they realize that He has never dropped them and He never will. When I was growing up, my finances were simple. Mom and dad took care of all the heavy lifting, while I did some basic chores and got an allowance. That allowance was typically spent on Pogs, which were super popular at the time, or some other random fun. Pretty simple. I never had to worry about breakfast, what was in my sack lunch for school, or if dinner would be on the table. I had a good father who worked hard to bring home the bacon and an incredible cook for a mom. I knew I was going to be taken care of so I never developed an orphan mindset.

I know that orphaned children in the world is an extremely sad reality, but perhaps even more sad is that the orphan mindset is plaguing the minds of believers who aren't convinced that they have a good Father. They believe that Jesus was good enough to save but somehow the Father that provided the greatest gift of His Son won't meet their other needs. It is silly to think that God is capable of meeting the need for salvation but not for rent. Jehovah Jireh provides lavishly! His greatest demonstration of provision was at the cross. Every other act of provision is lesser when compared to the provision of the cross. The religious leaders of Jesus' day didn't kill Jesus, the Father killed Jesus. It was His will. Jesus chose to be obedient to the will of the Father. Nobody took His life from Him; He laid it down on His own accord because the Father willed it. The Father's commitment to providing for the greatest need of humanity was fulfilled through the cross.

Whatever need you currently have, look at it through the scope of the Father's capability of provision and that need will suddenly shrink. I am not saying that the need suddenly goes away, but when you put your faith in a good Father who clearly provides for His children, a confidence begins to rise. "I don't know how I'm going to pay off these bills…but Father, You're good and You've got this." "I don't know how I'm going to pay this month's rent…but Father, You're good and You've got this." "I can't seem to hold down a good relationship that pleases you as I hope to get married…but Father, You're good and You've got this." "I don't know what my future looks like and my career keeps changing…but Father, You're good and You've got this." Lean into Him. He knows what He's doing.

In 2012, the Lord spoke very clearly to my wife about leaving her career with a federal job to go full-time in ministry with me. We were very excited because the Lord had spoken so clearly to us but we were about to begin a faith journey in the area of our finances. She was making a lot more money than I was as a youth pastor, and we were still freshly married living in a condo in north county San Diego. Our finances were easily cut by 60 percent. Financially speaking, this made no sense. If I spent the time pondering all the reasons why God was saying this, I probably would have convinced myself that it wasn't Him speaking. I would have talked myself out of the future blessings of God due to my inability to trust in His voice. If His sheep really know His voice we'll make moves whenever the Shepherd, Jehovah Ra'ah, commands anything.

Then the Lord spoke to me right after we made this decision and told me that He wanted me to continue tithing as if Ashley was still working. Well that was now more than double what we were already giving and with the income shrinking, it didn't make a lot of sense. But I knew what I heard from the Lord so we decided to be obedient. Our accounts began a steady decline month after month as we prayed and trusted God to make provision. For months, nothing drastic seemed to happen. We finally got to the point where we weren't sure how we were going to make next month's rent. I remember holding Ashley on our kitchen floor as she cried and cried.

It is during these moments that our faith is truly put to the test. I am sure she began to wonder if we had made the right decision, though in her heart she knew we had, but there was no answer to our prayers in sight. In that moment I felt such a thrust of faith within me I just held my wife and told her, "God's got this. He's gonna take care of us. He knows what He's doing." In the coming days, I admit even my faith was beginning to get a little shaky, but I remember striving to hold my ground in faith, believing that we were nearer to our moment of breakthrough than we had ever been before.

God is a dramatic God. The children of Israel could have come over the hill leaving Egypt on their way to the Promised Land and when they saw the Red Sea, it could have already been split down the middle and it would have been clear that this was the direction God wanted them to go. But noooooooooooooo…God is a dramatic God! The most powerful army in the world was chasing them, fire was falling from Heaven keeping them away from the Israelites, Moses stepped into that water full of faith with his staff in hand and thrust it into the waters as it split right down the middle. Then the fires were sucked back into Heaven as the Egyptians were released to chase them down into the seabed, only to be moments too late to catch them as the water walls come crashing in on them. God is a dramatic God.

Ashley and I felt like we were up against a Red Sea and needing a supernatural intervention, quickly. Then, through a series of miracles…in our darkest moment…God supernaturally brought to us eleven thousand dollars out of nowhere! Random checks started showing up in our mailbox from people sending us money for no reason and who knew nothing about our situation. Ashley got into a minor car accident that totaled our car, even though it was just a small dent in the door. We received thousands in insurance money and were able to fix the car and pocket the money. We found a random check in our glove box that had been there for who knows how long and it was still a valid check. Our tax return was far larger than we anticipated. We were planning to move out of our condo and in with some family and right when we were about to mention to our landlord that we were going to leave, he contacted us and to tell us that he sold the property and he unfortunately had to ask us to vacate the condo. Since we were being asked to leave, we were compensated thousands of dollars.

Miracle after miracle happened over the course of four weeks and God split the sea in front of us and led us through on dry ground. Jehovah Jireh was manifesting His goodness to us in dramatic fashion. This is only one story of many. Now when I am facing a financial predicament, my confidence in Jehovah Jireh is on another level. Since I have seen the provisional characteristic of a good Father so vividly so many times, my faith for Him to take care of us is strong. I choose to remember what He did the last time we were standing on the shores of a Red Sea believing for the waters to split and Jehovah Jireh showed up.

Since learning this lesson I've seen God come through again and again. Not just in dramatic moments when we find ourselves in a financial dilemma, but in moments where He just felt like giving to us because He loves us. When looking to purchase a new SUV for our growing family, He blessed us with $17,000 to put as a down payment for it! We were then able to get a safer, newer, more reliable vehicle that will last our family for years to come. We thought the hospital bill for the delivery of our daughter Emma was going to be a particular amount and it ended up being 5 times as much which left us a bit worried. This was unexpected. That night we prayed to Jehovah Jireh to take care of us like He always had and then that very next day, we discovered money in an account from an old job I'd worked at almost a decade ago. The amount was almost to the dollar what we needed to pay the hospital! When we called the hospital to pay it in full, they cut the bill by about 30% which meant the money provided by the Lord wouldn't just pay the bill in full, but leave us with extra to help thrust us forward with our new baby. The stories go on and on. Some big and some small. All carrying the fingerprint of my Provider.

When Jesus taught how to pray, one of the crucial pieces to that prayer was: **"Give us this day our daily bread." (Matt. 6:11 NKJV).** In other words, God knows the needs of today and how to meet them. Jesus threw into the model prayer a reminder that Jehovah Jireh should be on your mind daily. He is constantly working out provisions for His kids.

I feel like so many people are stressing over their finances. We live in a society that demands we work hard and have high paying jobs to get by. I live in San Diego and it's very much true out here. But just because the demands are high doesn't mean that our stress levels have to be high. You'll find yourself stressing if you are the provider for your home. If you're not, then it's not your problem. I'm the only one who works in my home right now and that may not always be the case, but for now it is. It allows my wife to be a stay-at-home-mom to our amazing kids in a crucial time of their lives. I praise God for it! We're not lazy. Nor are we bad stewards of our finances. I know that I have to work and I work hard. I also pull side jobs and look for extra opportunities to bring in finances when the Lord guides those decisions. I never sit back on the couch with a cup of iced tea and let Jehovah Jireh handle my mess. It's a partnership. He most often provides for my family through me. I'm also not constantly on the hunt for those side jobs, hoping to make enough extra money to get by. That would once again be me trying to play the provider roll in the home. He's the Provider, and I simply partner with Him in the process. There is a key difference.

My understanding of this has rendered me free from anxiety. We never miss a meal. We have nice clothes and a wonderful home. We have toys and gadgets to play with. We have date night each week and so many more wonderful blessings. Why? Because, He is my Provider and He is yours too. Blessings in your life may look different than they do in mine. We cannot compare ourselves to each other. I could easily complain that my house isn't big enough, my cars aren't fast enough, my clothes aren't new enough, my bank account isn't full enough, especially when compared to others. But I refuse to take the burden of being provider of my house away from Him. He's all too good at it and I'm far too happy without that stress.

We have kept this mindset when financially we feel stable and when we've survived off of government assistance plus $400 a month. God took care of us through seasons of need and through seasons of plenty. Apparently the apostle Paul had the same story and he alludes to it in his letter to the church at Philippi: "**Not that I was ever in need, for I have learned how to be content with whatever I have. I know how to live on almost nothing or with everything. I have learned the secret of living in every situation, whether it is with a full stomach or empty, with plenty or little" (Phil. 4:11-12 NLT).**

This should encourage you. A full bank account doesn't make you rich. An empty bank account doesn't make you poor. I would argue that in many ways, Paul was one of the richest men on the planet and yet the Lord took him through seasons living on almost nothing. Even Jesus had to borrow a coin to make an illustration. He even told Peter to catch a fish and pull the coin out of its mouth to pay their taxes. If He's supernatural enough to know there would somehow be a coin in the fish's mouth valuable enough to pay the taxes for both of them, why doesn't He just materialize it right then out of thin air? He was establishing a principle to Peter and to the rest of the world. He'll provide, but only through our partnership with Him. Peter still had to use his skills as a fisherman, his trade, to go get that fish. So don't be surprised if God directs you or I to utilize our skills or trade to bring in finances when there is a need.

Know this friends, God's got it. Jehovah Jireh knows how to meet your need. Let faith arise inside of your hearts and believe that He is a good Father Who always takes care of His kids. Sometimes His provision doesn't look like how you want it to look, but that's because He might be meeting a greater need that you didn't even realize you had. So trust Him. Lean into Him. He is the best Daddy around and it's His good pleasure to provide for His children.

15
POWERFUL ATTENTION

Once for my birthday, my wife took me on a scenic tour boat around San Diego with my family. After we docked, we began walking back to our vehicle along the boardwalk. There was lots of activity along the boardwalk since this was a heavy tourist part of San Diego. There was a man there singing some worship songs on a cheap PA system. I admired his boldness, but we just walked on by. My wife and I are passionate lovers of Jesus, the same God that he was praising through that microphone, but he would have never known it because we simply walked on by. We started talking about why we were so disinterested in this guy. It's not like he was doing anything wrong. Perhaps it was because it was a little cheesy. Perhaps it was because, well to be honest, he wasn't the best singer. Or perhaps it was because there really wasn't much to draw us to him. Nothing that made us really want to go talk with him or find out more about why he was out there singing. We wondered…what would have made us stop? What would have captured our attention? What would have stopped us dead in our tracks and stimulated our curiosity? After much discussion, we both landed on a remarkable truth that a demonstration of power would have really attracted us. We concluded that if there were genuine demonstrations of power in authority we would stop everything to participate in what was happening on that boardwalk. We would change our plans, inconvenience our kids, risk getting a ticket for staying past the allotted time on a parking meter and who knows what else in order to be a part of God's obvious power moving in our midst.

Power is attractive. Power captivates the attention of people. Ministries all around the nation are always trying to pull another rabbit out of the hat in order to keep the attention of the people because most ministries are void of power. If we walked in the power that Jesus provided for us through His precious Holy Spirit, we wouldn't have to work so hard to keep the attention of the people. But if we don't move in that power, it's no wonder why we are left with planning the next stunt hopefully worthy enough to get people to come back next week.

Now, I love entertainment. I love media, drama, production and all that, but not nearly as much as the tangible power of God. One excites me for a moment, the other changes me for a lifetime. It is sad that so many churches feel the burden to attempt to put on a more impressive show than the church down the street in order to get the people to choose their church over another's. So pastors become circus performers instead of shepherds. Teachers anointed with the Spirit of God who are enabled to change the circumstances of those hurting all around them are reduced to comedians, story-tellers, and motivational speakers.

That burden is too great for us to bear. Very few have the means to keep up with today's entertainment driven society. We are usually ten years behind what's happening in Hollywood, underfunded and wildly less excellent. If you're attempting to grow your ministry or church, I believe *an* answer is found in the power of God. Host Him well and keep that your priority; people will be drawn to the place that power surges from. I know this is hard to get on board with for some of us. It is hard for me if I am honest. It's difficult to know the answer to what my ministry needs, and I battle seeing it not manifest consistently. Within our young adult ministry, we make room for the power of God to move. We've seen Him do some incredible things in our midst but it's nowhere near what I believe is coming. I know, with all my heart, that this is what the Father is breathing on and always has been. So my results or circumstances don't change this truth for me. I will continue to pray, believe, and provoke others to muster up their faith alongside me. This very book you're reading is a sign to me that I believed well even before the full manifestation of the power breakout was released in my life. I'm excited to say that when it was sprinkling, we celebrated the rain that would soon come. Just because the full outpouring hadn't been released yet, all the qualities of rain were already in our midst. I know a day will come when His power will move through us unlike ever before, and I'm confident that my belief system for that power in that degree will be very similar to how it is in this degree. So, we'll keep making room for His power in our gatherings. Not only will we make room, we will prepare and believe for His power to be present as we pull on that reality by our faith and actions. When headaches leave and when cancerous tumors fall off. When back pain lessons and when the dead are raised. I simply believe His Word to be true and the ministry of Jesus is my standard.

There are certain things we see that forever change us. That memory becomes seared into our minds and memories and it molds who we are as a person. I was recently having lunch with my pastor, Brian Ross, and he told me a story of some horrific things he saw in Calcutta. What he saw changed him. He can still remember the vivid, terrible sights and smells that burned into his memory. He told me, "Even as I explain the story now it doesn't do it justice...you won't be impacted by it like how I was impacted by it because I was there. It changes a person when they see certain things." If a powerful horrific experience can forever change a person, perhaps a powerful beautiful experience can change a person for the

128

better. I wonder what power encounters are awaiting us. Perhaps when we experience them, it'll change our everyday lives or at the very least, mark us from that day forward.

I know that by simply seeing a miracle, it doesn't save me or provoke me to change. Hundreds of people saw Jesus perform miracles and they were never changed. They were attracted to Him because power is attractive but that doesn't mean they were changed.

My dad was once driving to a meeting when he felt the Holy Spirit direct him to turn around and go pray for a 90-year-old family member who was in the hospital. She had a terminal cancerous tumor on her chest that restricted her swallowing. She was about to get a stent put in to open her esophagus so she could swallow again. Then she was to be sent home basically to die. My dad went into that hospital room full of faith, knowing that God wouldn't send him there for no reason. He prayed for her that night and then left without any sign that anything had happened. Two days later, while prepping her for the stent, the surgeons simply couldn't find the cancer. They took more x-rays, only to discover it had miraculously disappeared and all life threatening symptoms reversed, resulting in her living for almost ten more years!

That day the doctors and nurses were testifying all around the hospital that a miracle had happened. Our family was buzzing off of what God had done. What seemed like a revival swept through the family. Those who were far from God now had a desire for Bible studies and couldn't stop talking about what God had done. Unfortunately, this lasted for only a short time. Then slowly but surely, those excited family members forgot about what God had done and their faith began fading away. Seeing the still walking, breathing miracle right before their very eyes wasn't enough to change their lives. It attracted them to Him, but that's not enough. They have a decision to make once they find Jesus. Pastor Brian Ross once said, "We're saved by grace, but we're changed by choice." Discovering Him isn't enough. Making Him Lord and Savior is everything.

I believe that the activity of God cultivates the soil of people's hearts. Likely the most impactful sermon ever preached was the Sermon on the Mount recorded in Matthew chapters 5-7. Most scholars agree that this wasn't just one sermon but a series of sermons that Jesus preached over several days. There were massive crowds in attendance to hear Jesus teach what is commonly known as The Beatitudes. It's about the perspective believers should have in order to see the Kingdom of God and so much more. Jesus is essentially teaching how to live in order to see the Kingdom of God manifest in your life.

Before Jesus taught this incredible lesson to the people for multiple days, He had to make sure their hearts were cultivated so the seeds He was about to sow would land on good soil. The end of Matthew 4 shows us how Jesus prepared their heart soil for the Sermon on the Mount:

> **Jesus traveled throughout the region of Galilee, teaching in the synagogues and announcing the Good News about the Kingdom. And he healed every kind of disease and illness. News about him spread as far as Syria, and people soon began bringing to him all who were sick. And whatever their sickness or disease, or if they were demon possessed or epileptic or paralyzed–he healed them all. Large crowds followed him wherever he went– people from Galilee, the Ten Towns,**

Jerusalem, from all over Judea, and from east of the Jordan River. (Matt. 4:23-25 NLT)

Jesus prepared the people to hear what He was about to say, by doing what only He could do. Demonstrate the Kingdom, gain the attention of the people, then preach the Kingdom to a ready captivated audience. He healed every kind of disease and illness. When the sick and demonized were brought to Him, He healed them all! Jesus captured the attention of the people through the demonstration of power. He was preparing the soil for the seeds of the Kingdom.

Paul, the apostle, is preaching away, late into the night. I'm sure those listening are eager to hear what he has to say but as minutes turn to hours the brain starts to fry. The story is found in Acts chapter 20: **"As Paul spoke on and on, a young man named Eutychus, sitting on the windowsill, became very drowsy. Finally, he fell sound asleep and dropped three stories to his death below. Paul went down, bent over him, and took him into his arms. 'Don't worry,' he said, 'he's alive!' Then they all went back upstairs, shared in the Lord's Supper, and ate together. Paul continued talking to them until dawn, and then he left" (Acts 20:9-11 NLT).**

I'm certain the attention of the people was far greater after the boy was resurrected. The power released validates the message released. Interestingly, the boy's name, Eutychus, means "fortunate or lucky." What a fitting name. Had he have been listening to a preacher void of the power of God, he would have been dead for certain. If I would have been the preacher that night, would the boy still be considered fortunate?

Nobody can focus on what we have to say when they are physically dying. People cannot see their spiritual need

131

when they are blinded by their massive physical need. Hope is eclipsed by a mountain of pain and suffering. They need a conduit of power to remove the mountain in front of them so they can receive the greater spiritual blessing awaiting them. We carry that power. Romans 8:11 NLT states, **"The Spirit of God, who raised Jesus from the dead, lives in you. And just as God raised Christ Jesus from the dead, he will give life to your mortal bodies by this same Spirit living within you."**

The *same* Spirit that raised Him from the dead. The *same* power that raised Jesus from the dead is in us. This seriously blows my mind. We seem to have no doubt believing that we'll catch a virus from a sick person, but no faith believing that a person can catch the greater power that we carry. What if the enemy didn't want us shaking hands with anybody under his dominion because if we did, what's in us would get on them and things would start rearranging within them?

We all want to preach the truth to the lost and teach about the wonderful things of God, but when we do, those seeds often fall on unprepared soil at best. Jesus was about to spend the next several days teaching on the Kingdom of God and Kingdom lifestyle, so He prepared the soil of the people by captivating their attention with demonstrations of power. When Christians move in power, it is not to draw attention to themselves, it is to draw attention to the source of that power: Almighty God. A magician, through illusion, can make a helicopter disappear or other seemingly unbelievable acts and then they will always pause for applause once the climax of their trick is reached. A healthy Christian should demonstrate the power of God and simultaneously disappear from any offer of glory. It is the difference between us and the world. The glory of the showman is the applause and recognition; the glory of the

Christian is the smile of approval from their Father in Heaven.

After healing the paralyzed man at the gate called Beautiful, Peter addresses the people saying, **"…'People of Israel,' he said, 'what is so surprising about this? And why stare at us as though we had made this man walk by our own power or godliness?'" (Acts 3:12 NLT).** Peter is saying, don't look at us as if we did this on our own. We are just conduits of power given to us by Jesus through His Holy Spirit. Set your eyes on Jesus, He is the Healer!

There is a fascinating story in the book of Judges about a seemingly insignificant man named Gideon. He was an Israelite, and his people were being horribly oppressed by the Midianites to the point of starvation. Gideon was threshing wheat in a winepress which is strange within itself. You thresh wheat on a threshing floor and press grapes at a winepress. But since the Midianites knew that Israel was barely surviving, they were confident none of them would be at the winepress, which is where the drink of celebration is made. At that time, there wasn't anything to celebrate in the Israelite camp. Gideon was doing this to hide the grain from the Midianites. Here's what happened:

> **The angel of the LORD appeared to him and said, "Mighty hero, the LORD is with you!"**
>
> **"Sir," Gideon replied, "if the LORD is with us, why has all this happened to us? And where are all the miracles our ancestors told us about? Didn't they say, 'The LORD brought us up out of Egypt'? But now the LORD has abandoned us and handed us over to the Midianites." (Judg. 6:12 -13 NLT)**

Hold up! What in the world was Gideon doing that

was so mighty? Gideon was hiding, and this angel called him a mighty hero. Was this angel of the LORD simply prophesying greatness into Gideon or was there something that Gideon was doing that positioned him to be this mighty hero?

Judges 6:14-15 NLT continues, **"Then the LORD turned to him and said, 'Go with the strength you have, and rescue Israel from the Midianites. I am sending you!'**
'But Lord,' Gideon replied, 'how can I rescue Israel? My clan is the weakest in the whole tribe of Manasseh, and I am the least in my entire family!'"

Gideon was again showing this angel that he was obviously not the best choice for this mission to deliver Israel from the oppression of the Midianites. But this angel kept calling out this greatness within Gideon. Take a look again at verse 13: Gideon says, **"If the LORD is with us, why has all this happened to us? And where are all the miracles our ancestors told us about? Didn't they say, 'The LORD brought us up out of Egypt'?"** I believe this is where Gideon's strength was hidden. Gideon had a miracle mindset. If God is with us, there should be miracles! He is a miracle working God. Gideon grew up hearing about the Red Sea parting, fire falling from Heaven, water pouring forth from a rock, manna every morning, and so many other incredible miracles. Then he found himself in this difficult scenario and he was beginning to wonder where the God of his people was. That is a valid argument. Since there were no miracles, there was obviously no presence of God around. I believe the LORD saw this as a radical strength in Gideon.

If you read the rest of this amazing story, you'll discover how God partners with Gideon, thins out his army, and delivers them from oppression. God made it abundantly clear that it was His strength working through man's weakness to make impossible things happen. The strength that man possessed in this story is his ability to believe that God can still do anything. He is the God of the miraculous.

This provokes me to take this miracle mindset into my day-to-day life. If God is with me, there should be miracles. Clearly, we don't make pursuing miracles the mission of our lives. We pursue God. We hunger for His will to be done in the earth. The miraculous simply happens all around God because He is supernatural. There was a strength found in Gideon when he believed that God can do all things; I believe we need this same strength coursing through our veins today.

We have a power strip at our house that has its own battery source within it. Its purpose is to plug your desktop computer into it or other electronics so that if there is a power outage, those electronics will continue running until the power comes back on. Whenever it gets unplugged or the power goes out, it makes this horrible beeping sound that doesn't stop until it is reconnected to the power. We need this spiritually. We need to walk in such nearness to the Lord that an alarm goes off when we are not connected to the power. Connectivity to the power is essential to the life of anybody who wants to live like Jesus. Why? Because, we should want the seeds we sow to fall on good soil. We want to capture the attention of the people so that their hearts are ready to receive what the Spirit is saying to them. Furthermore, we want to carry the solution to the hurting people all around us. We don't just want to talk to them, we want to demonstrate the love and power of God to them.

Jesus put so much stock in the demonstration of power that He said, **"Don't believe me unless I carry out my Father's work. But if I do His work, believe in the evidence of the miraculous works I have done, even if**

you don't believe me. Then you will know and understand that the Father is in me, and I am in the Father" (John 10:37-38 NLT).

That's bold! Jesus gave His listeners an out. If they didn't see Him carrying out the works of the Father in power, they didn't have to believe anything He had to say. This inspires me. I want to be so confident in the power that is within me that I wouldn't teach unless the soil of people's hearts were ready. That is how Jesus did it. He trusted His encounters with people to be enough to forever change them.

Jesus sails to the region of the Gadarenes to personally encounter one man in Luke chapter 8. A demonized man so vexed by devils he's living in the tombs, cutting himself with rocks, naked and unable to be restrained by any chains; he's a menace to society. Jesus sets him free from the legion of demons within him and the townspeople come out to find him seated, clothed, and in his right mind. It is such a radical shift from his previous status that the townspeople are freaking out. The freshly delivered man asks Jesus if he can continue to follow Him, but Jesus so trusted this man's encounter with Him that He denied him to continue along with Him. Of all the people that needed some additional attention, this guy was probably at the top of the list. Still, Jesus sent him on to tell the region about the wonderful thing God had done for him. No seminary. No special training. No ten-step program. Simply, one encounter with the power of God, through Jesus.

We need the power of God. If we're to accurately portray Jesus to the world around us, we need His power. If we're to effectively love the world around us, we need His power. If we're to capture the attention of the world, it won't be through what we're currently doing. This apparently is not working well. I'm convinced that we need the power of God.

16
FIVE-SENSE ENCOUNTERS

Our five senses are God's idea. I believe that He desires for us to experience Him through each of our five senses. Let's just think about this for a moment. We're created in His image, and everything He has created is also to be enjoyed by His creation. A lion could enjoy lying down in the shade of a tree. A dolphin could enjoy a swim in the ocean. A dog could run through the tall grass in an open field. A human can enjoy an ice-cream on a hot day, the companionship of a friend, the music of a skilled artist, and endless other possibilities. Just about everything that can be experienced in this world can be "sensed" through our five senses. Why not God? What a waste these senses would be if we couldn't experience the One who created them with them.

The Scriptures are filled with people who encountered God, and if we see the Scriptures as permission for what's available to us today, as we should, we are encouraged to also experience God. He is a real Person, not some imaginary thought. If I had to live satisfied with the fact my wife simply exists somewhere but I never got to experience her company, I would be at a huge loss. I would also argue that my love for my imaginary wife would not be nearly as strong as my love for her that developed through experience. The very fact that we get to be together catapults our love one for another to greater levels. The same is true with God. The more we experience Him, the more we fall in love with Him.

Many people don't have much issue with experiencing God through *some* of our senses but just not all of them. On the other hand, some people have put too much stock into experiencing God. Others have cast experience aside altogether, wasting away a wonderful means of love increase for God through those encounters that He's made available. What I have discovered is those who don't have encounters with God, or very rarely do, are frustrated with those who do have frequent encounters with God. Their experiences differ. The one who has no encounters begins to formulate ideas or even unrighteous thoughts towards those who have experiences and enjoy them. In many cases, it is essentially envy. Both deep down want encounters with Him. Since one is not experiencing encounters, they justify away why it's not happening and then condemn the other who is having encounters. The individual not having encounters can choose to either be offended or provoked. If he chooses offense, then he'll never be stimulated to walk in encounters with God and write off those who do experience God in that way as "weird," "super-spiritual," "hyper-Pentecostal," or something of the like.

Since this is no new thing, theological stances are already prepared for this type of thinking. Some people might say, "experiencing God is not for today. We don't need encounters with God, we just need His saving grace. What good does an encounter do? I already love Jesus just like I am." All one would need to do is look at the Bible and allow that to be our starting point for what is acceptable and encouraged for us today. If the individual who isn't having encounters with God chooses to be provoked instead of offended, a whole world of opportunity opens up to him. He allows the experiences of others to light a fire of possibility inside of him. He may then read the Scriptures and begin believing that if God would speak that way with Moses, perhaps He would speak that way with him. A seed of pursuit, planted in the soil of wonder begins to germinate. A mindset shift takes place and that individual says, "If God is not a respecter of persons, and He did that for him, I wonder if He'll do it for me too?"

The Word of God is full of permissions. If Elijah experienced it, so can I! If Moses saw it, why can't I? If Jesus lived that way, shouldn't I strive for the same? This is the stance I have chosen. When I hear a speaker at a conference or talk with somebody experiencing God in a way that I haven't yet, I let that testimony create a seed of opportunity in me. If I nurture that seed and let it fall on good soil, it provokes me to strive for the same. I may not like every little thing that person says, but I choose to eat the meat and spit out the bones. You may not be very excited about this chapter thus far, but if you honestly knew you could experience God through your five senses wouldn't you want to? I pray you're provoked.

I was recently in a conversation with someone who shared a story with me that challenged me. This person shared a story of a Heavenly experience. It was full of detail and wonderment. As I listened to the story I could feel my emotions stirring. I literally had tears fall from my eyes. I smiled ear to ear. I was like a child listening to their favorite fairy tale again. Only this story, I know to be a reality. Even though I didn't understand everything that was told to me, I chose not to be offended. I simply let the possibilities stir within me.

We cannot afford to lower our standard to personal experiences. There is much more permitted to us when Jesus stated, **"I tell you the truth, anyone who believes in me will do the same works I have done, and even greater works, because I am going to be with the Father" (John 14:12 NLT).** We are enabled to do even greater works than Jesus did because He went to the Father. That reference to Him going to the Father is paramount in relation to us because He went to the Father so that He could send the Holy Spirit to us. Which goes back to what we have already talked a lot about; we have the Holy Spirit living within us, enabling us to live a life of victory and to reach others through supernatural power. Just because something hasn't happened to us doesn't mean that it doesn't happen. Furthermore, there are several key verses in Scripture like the one in John 14:12 that leave lots of room for possibilities. Who knows what those greater works look like? Who knows what all Jesus did that if they were written down all the books of the world couldn't contain them like it says in John 21:25? I think it's a real shame to diminish the possibilities of God down to our personal experiences. He is just so much bigger than that.

Let's explore through our five senses and see what Biblical backing we can find for them.

Sight: Aside from Jesus walking the earth, the Bible is filled with references of people seeing into the spiritual realm. Encounters with angels and God Himself. After Jacob wrestled with an angel who many believe was actually the Son of God, he said, **"Jacob named the place Peniel (which means 'face of God'), for he said, 'I have seen God face to face, yet my life has been spared'" (Gen. 32:30 NLT).**

Prophets were taken into incredible visions where they saw Heavenly things, unheard of beings, impossible to describe places, and so much more. Not to mention after Jesus' resurrection He appeared to so many people! I see the results of God working all around me all the time but only once have I seen Jesus. It was in a powerful dream I had and let's just say Jesus was so full of joy. It was almost as if He had been waiting to reveal Himself to me in that manner. It was beautiful! An encounter with Him I'd been waiting for that I will never forget. Rest assured, we can

141

surely see God. There is overwhelming Scriptural evidence of seeing God.

Hearing: Most people don't have any problem with knowing that God can speak to them. Still, the most accepted way people hear from God is through His Word or by somebody else prophetically speaking. But can God actually speak to us? I've never personally audibly heard the voice of God, but I know for a fact I have heard Him time and time again in other ways. He literally spoke to several people all throughout Scripture. Just to name a couple, we will simply only look at the book of Genesis:

Noah-

"Then God said, 'I am giving you a sign of my covenant with you and with all living creatures, for all generations to come'" (Gen. 9:12 NLT).

Abraham-

"The LORD had said to Abram, 'Leave your native country, your relatives, and your father's family, and go to the land that I will show you. I will make you into a great nation. I will bless you and make you famous, and you will be a blessing to others. I will bless those who bless you and curse those who treat you with contempt. All the families on earth will be blessed through you'" (Gen. 12:1-3 NLT).

Sarah-

"Sarah was afraid, so she denied it, saying, 'I didn't laugh.' But the LORD said, 'No, you did laugh'" (Gen. 18:15 NLT).

Jacob-

"During the night God spoke to him in a vision. 'Jacob! Jacob!' he called.
'Here I am,' Jacob replied.

'I am God, the God of your father,' the voice said. 'Do not be afraid to go down to Egypt, for there I will

make your family into a great nation'" (Gen. 46:2-3 NLT).

Those instances are amazing, and that's not to mention Moses whom God spoke with face to face as one who speaks to a friend. All of the prophets whom He spoke to constantly. Kings and leaders He spoke with. Who could forget Jesus Himself Whom God spoke to audibly at His baptism and on the mountain of transfiguration? Saul on the road to Damascus. John the beloved and so many others all throughout the Scriptures.

Touch: Here's where people start to get funky. Most don't have any problem with the fact that we can see God or hear from God but why do we need to touch Him? Why would He need to touch us? I agree, we should seek God for Who He is not just the hand of God. It is not about what He can do for us, it is about seeking Who He is as God. However, I do believe the touch from God comes as a secondary byproduct of seeking Him overall.

I have already told the story of my desperate pursuit of His touch and not finding it. But what I did find was the *pursuit* of the touch, which to me was far more valuable. There was a hunger built inside of me to keep pursuing the touch of God. I keep likening a relationship with God to that of a husband and a wife because I believe that relationship between husband and wife is the most intimate, oneness relationship we can experience, and that's the closest thing to our relationship with Him we can liken it too. But if I could only hear my wife and see my wife and never touch her, that would be a major bummer. There sure wouldn't be any Emma or Judah that's for certain! We are supposed to enjoy touching our spouse; He made us that way.

The same is true with Almighty God. I've personally had many encounters where I physically felt something supernatural happening to me; it was the touch of God. I

143

have felt that weighty presence of God in worship. Where the "kabowd"—glory of God—comes into the room and the atmosphere changes to a thick, enjoyable heaviness. It's that weighty presence of God you can actually feel. I have had dreams where I felt the power of God surging through my body. Where wonderful waves of power roll over me again and again. It's difficult to describe but it was most definitely sensational. I personally like that feeling I get when a roller coaster falls and my stomach leaps into my chest; these experiences were something like that. I have awoken in the middle of the night still gently vibrating or trembling in the presence of the Lord after an impactful God dream. I have been prayed over at services probably thousands of times throughout my life and the vast majority of the time I don't feel much at all. But there are a few times where the Spirit of God has LAID ME OUT!

I remember once getting called out on a Sunday morning and a guest speaker began praying for me from the stage as I stood in the aisle. The best way I can describe what happened was almost as if an angel was in the ceiling with a wrecking ball, and then he released it and suddenly BOOM! I go from standing still, eyes closed, quietly praying and receiving from the Lord through this prophetic word to flying back a good eight feet and crashing to the ground, unhurt. I remained on the ground for about 10 minutes, dazed and overwhelmed at the presence of God resting upon me as He just touched me powerfully upon the ground. It was gnarly to say the least. This has only happened to me perhaps one or two other times. When I got up off the floor, I was changed.

I've also gone to revival style meetings with powerful men of God ministering and felt nothing whatsoever. I remember being lined up shoulder to shoulder with other pastors from all over the region while Rodney Howard-

Browne laid hands on each of us. One by one people were overcome by the presence of God and were laid out on the floor. I was so full of expectancy; I couldn't wait for him to get to me. I knew God was going to blow me up (in a good way). Like dominos, everybody fell out; when he got to me…nothing. He prayed a moment longer for me…still nothing. Then he moved on and they kept falling out. I stood alone like the obvious sinner amongst all the pastors at the front of the room! It was so funny, in retrospect. I was still blessed that night, and I enjoyed the presence of the Lord, but I didn't feel a thing. I learned a great lesson that day: I don't have to feel anything. Sometimes God will touch me and it will be wonderful, and sometimes I'll simply enjoy the fact I know He's near. It doesn't matter either way. I should appreciate both.

Did that experience keep me from wanting a touch from God in the future? ABSOLUTELY NOT! I still go up to receive prayer and welcome whatever God decides to do to me physically. Sometimes I feel the touch from Him, sometimes I don't. It doesn't change my love for Him or His love for me. Do I want the touch from Him every time? Yes. It simply just doesn't always happen. But I'm going to keep going after Him with everything in me, and if He does choose to lay me out on the ground, then you'd better believe I am going to get up changed. Damon Thompson preaches it like this, "In the Scriptures, you weren't anointed because you could knock people down, you were anointed when you could lift people up! When cripples walked, and the paralyzed were set free. If something I cannot see knocks me to the ground, you'd better believe I'm going to get up radically different." We don't need to get slain in the Spirit ten more times; we need to experience Him so radically that one encounter with Him changes everything.

Here are some examples of people getting touched by God in Scripture:

Jacob-

"This left Jacob all alone in the camp, and a man came and wrestled with him until the dawn began to break. When the man saw that he would not win the match, he touched Jacob's hip and wrenched it out of its socket" (Gen. 32:24-25 NLT).

Isaiah-

"Then one of the seraphim flew to me with a burning coal he had taken from the altar with a pair of tongs. He touched my lips with it and said, 'See, this coal has touched your lips. Now your guilt is removed, and your sins are forgiven'" (Isa. 6:6-7 NLT).

Jeremiah-

Then the LORD reached out and touched my mouth and said, "Look, I have put my words in your mouth!'" (Jer. 1:9 NLT).

Daniel-

"While he was speaking to me, I looked down at the ground, unable to say a word. Then the one who looked like a man touched my lips, and I opened my mouth and began to speak. I said to the one standing in front of me, "I am filled with anguish because of the vision I have seen, my lord, and I am very weak. How can someone like me, your servant, talk to you, my lord? My strength is gone, and I can hardly breathe."

Then the one who looked like a man touched me again, and I felt my strength returning. (Dan. 10:15-18 NLT)

Jesus touched thousands of people and miracles took place. Even after Jesus' resurrection, He still touched people and people touched Him like Thomas. Throughout the book of Acts, thousands more experienced a touch of God through His Holy Spirit.

I honestly believe He wants to touch you. But, I also believe He knows what He is doing and He doesn't want to shake your faith or derail you. Therefore, He gives you what you can handle. But also, like we've mentioned several times already, He responds to faith. So, asking Him for a touch might just move His hands.

Taste: In the middle of a beautiful time of worship, I have had friends who said they could taste something sweet invading their taste buds in their mouth. Testifying that it tasted like honey or some other sweet substance. I have only had a couple instances in my personal life where I felt like I tasted something that I certainly wasn't eating or drinking, but to be honest, it wasn't so overwhelming to me that I started telling people about it. However, if we look at Scripture, we do find a couple instances that give some clues to this possibility. **"Oh, taste and see that the LORD *is* good; Blessed *is* the man *who* trusts in Him!" (Psa. 34:8 NKJV).**

Tasting and seeing God's goodness. I like that David puts both tasting and seeing together. Once again, many people would have no problem with seeing that God is good but have great difficulty with tasting His goodness. He could have chosen many other words to describe simply experiencing God's goodness, but he chose to taste Him as well. Every other major translation also translates this word as taste, because, I believe, that's actually what David meant. Surely God can provide food for the hungry and out of that goodness the recipient is tasting His goodness. That of course makes sense, but it does not diminish the possibility of actually sensing through taste the lovely goodness of God.

Here are some more Scriptures to chew on:

Psalm 119:103 NLT states, **"How sweet your words taste to me; they are sweeter than honey."**

Metaphorical? Maybe. Literal? Maybe.

Ezekiel was once in a radical encounter with the Lord and God said:

"The voice said to me, 'Son of man, eat what I am giving you—eat this scroll! Then go and give its message to the people of Israel.' So I opened my mouth, and he fed me the scroll. 'Fill your stomach with this,' he said. And when I ate it, it tasted as sweet as honey in my mouth" (Ezek. 3:1-3 NLT).

A similar instance happened to John in Revelation:

"So I went to the angel and told him to give me the small scroll. 'Yes, take it and eat it,' he said. 'It will be sweet as honey in your mouth, but it will turn sour in your stomach!' So I took the small scroll from the hand of the angel, and I ate it! It was sweet in my mouth, but when I swallowed it, it turned sour in my stomach" (Rev. 10:9-10 NLT). Both of those stories are separated by hundreds and hundreds of years chronologically speaking. But they are strikingly similar.

Hopefully these stories and Scriptures create an appetite for you to consider that God can indeed be tasted. This is not a wasted sense, doomed to never experience God.

My dad was once pouring into a new believer and he was talking about "eating the Word of God," and this new believer didn't understand the metaphor, so he literally started tearing pages out of the Bible and eating them. That dude took tasting the Word to another level. I highly do not recommend this. Especially if your Bible is a smartphone...please don't eat your phone!

Smell: There is literally a fragrance of God. You can't buy it at Macy's or Amazon.com. In fact, the only place you can get it is in the presence of the One whom the fragrance emanates from. I can remember worshipping Jesus at a service and smelling this wonderfully soft, but strong, almost vanilla-like incense fill the room. It remained for several minutes and then lifted. I wasn't sure who else was smelling it or if it was just me. My first thought was that somebody was putting on some fragrance of their own, using lotion or perfume of some kind. But that fragrance lingered for quite a while, far more than any typical fragrance lingers when somebody applies it to their skin. I even looked around me and nobody was putting anything on; they were all worshiping Jesus just like I was. Then the speaker got up and started mentioning how he too could smell that fragrance of the Lord in the room. He was standing far away from where I was which only further convinced me that the fragrance I was smelling was supernatural.

Recently on our young adult's service night I walked out of the door to the room we meet in and I stopped dead in my tracks. I could smell a strong fragrance of a fire burning. I walked to the fence line to see if I could see smoke burning close by but I saw nothing. In fact, I couldn't even smell the fire by the fence. Yet, it remained strong in front of the door to the room. I sent the custodian on duty to check the rest of the church and find the fire that was burning somewhere. Some time went by and I texted him asking him where the fire was. He replied there wasn't any fire. Interesting. I preached out of Acts chapter 10 and ended with the believers at Cornelius's house getting baptized in the Holy Spirit and fire. While preaching, the fire alarm went off upstairs from the room we were meeting it. Those working childcare that night even brought the kids down to our level because they weren't sure if it was a false alarm or a real fire. Those of us in the room never heard the fire alarm, we just kept preaching on the fire of God unaware of the commotion upstairs from us. We transitioned into worship and praying for people to be baptized in the Holy Spirit and fire while praying for the fire of God to burn in us unlike ever before. Several were refilled with the Spirit, some were baptized in fire for the first time. A visitor rededicated his life to Jesus which he hadn't done since he was twelve years old. Several on my team spent adequate time crying out for the fire of God to burn greater in them than ever before. It was easily top ten of our best services we've ever hosted. I later investigated to see if anybody had any fires going nearby and nobody did. Unless I'm missing something, that fire myself and several others smelled, and perhaps even that fire alarm that went off were natural responses to what God was doing spiritually. Impossible? Coincidence? Perhaps not.

There is plenty of Scripture to back up this type of experience. Let's look at some:

But thank God! He has made us his captives and continues to lead us along in Christ's triumphal procession. Now he uses us to spread the knowledge of Christ everywhere, like a sweet perfume. Our lives are a Christ-like fragrance rising up to God. But this fragrance is perceived differently by those who are being saved and by those who are perishing. To those who are perishing, we are a dreadful smell of death and doom. But to those who are being saved, we are a life-giving perfume. And who is adequate for such a task as this? (2 Cor. 2:14-16 NLT)

It's true that there certainly is a fragrance originating from the lives of those who belong to Him. Paul's reference to Christ's triumphal procession is likened to a Roman triumphal procession. This victory parade took place after conquering an opposing army. Both the victors and the captives were a part of the procession. The fragrances of burning spices in celebration of the conquering nation were burning and both the victors and captives could smell it. To the victors, it was an aroma of victory. To the captives, it was the aroma of death. The fragrance of Christ, or the Gospel, is an aroma of life to those who have accepted it and chosen to breathe it into themselves. To those who have rejected it, it is the aroma of death, signifying their certain judgment. In the spiritual realm, I wonder if there is indeed an actual fragrance that is released from those who have accepted Christ and perhaps an actual stench upon those who have not.

Many have testified that after having encounters with the demonic realm they can smell the stench of burning sulfur and other horrific scents. This lines up with these Scriptures. It's funny to me that many believers have more faith to believe this awful type of smell coming into our natural realm than a glorious smell that comes from believers or from the realm of Heaven.

There are several Scriptures in Leviticus and Numbers that refer to offerings being presented to the Lord, and when they are burned, they are a soothing aroma to the Lord. That act of worship that created a literal aroma was pleasing to God.

Smelling the fragrance of our worship and prayer to the Lord is so enjoyable to God, He made one of the fundamental furnishings of His temple the altar of incense. This incense signified the prayers of the people to the Lord; it was a soothing aroma to Him. Psalm 141:2 NLT states, **"Accept my prayer as an incense offered to you, and my upraised hands as an evening offering."** Then, Revelation

5:8 NLT explains, **"And when he took the scroll, the four living beings and the twenty-four elders fell down before the Lamb. Each one had a harp, and they held gold bowls filled with incense, which are the prayers of God's people."**

Clearly some of these encounters are less common than others, but that doesn't make them unnecessary or impossible. I have far more stories on seeing, hearing, and touching God than I do tasting or smelling Him. This simply provokes me. God, I would like to taste more of You. I want to smell You more often. Awaken these senses in me.

My encouragement to you is this; experience God. In any and every way He chooses. Let the experiences and encounters of others provoke you to know Him better. Whether He chooses to let you see Him, hear Him, touch Him, taste Him, smell Him, or some other phenomenal way of encountering Him, simply allow Him to do things His way. Remain balanced and always be sure to seek after Him, not only the encounters. But when encounters do come, let those encounters fuel your fire of passionate love for Him. That's ultimately why I felt this was worth talking about. If you're convinced that He's able to do these things, then why not invite Him to do them in your life. You may discover that as a result, more encounters will come. If more encounters come, perhaps more understanding will manifest. If more understanding is gained, perhaps our love for Him will grow. Steward these encounters well. Celebrate when they happen. Give all the glory to God. Fall deeper in love.

17
Do It Again

When we hear what God has done in the life of another, it should create an appetite in us to see Him to do it again. Your story is powerful. Your testimony is perhaps your greatest weapon. The Hebrew word for testimony or witness is the word *ed*, meaning witness, testimony, or evidence of things. This word comes from the root word *uwd*, meaning to return, repeat, go about, or do again. So, at the very root of a testimony— something we have seen and experienced—there is imbedded an invitation for God to do it again. Each time we tell our story, it comes already threaded with a prophetic seed ready to fall on the good soil of the hearers for God to repeat that same wonderful thing.

If God has done something wonderful in your life, you owe it to the world around you to tell your story. It's more than some random empty story for others to hear. It's also more than the history of events that led you up to your current place in life. It is prophecy. Revelation 19:10 NKJV states, **"And I fell at his feet to worship him. But he said to me, 'See that you do not do that! I am your fellow servant, and of your brethren who have the testimony of Jesus. Worship God! For the testimony of Jesus is the spirit of prophecy.'"**

Jesus didn't have to verbally tell us to do something in order for us to get the gist that we should do it. Jesus was living out what we should do every single day. Jesus loved the unlovable. He was modeling and prophetically saying for every generation to come, "See what I'm doing…DO IT AGAIN!" When He healed, restored, forgave, taught, welcomed, prayed, honored, died…He was showing you and me how you do it. The excuse that Jesus could do the things He did and we can't because He is God and we are not is an invalid excuse. In His divinity; He limited Himself to humanity, the same ingredients each of us will have so that we can actually do all that He did. This was one of His great purposes in the earth. To perfectly live in obedience to the Father, proving we could do the same. His testimony gives me permission to do likewise.

When I read the Scriptures, I read them through the lens of permission-granting. I love to pull all the best qualities of each character in Scripture and aim to apply them to my life. Obviously, Jesus is the best One to do this with, but there is so much we could pull from others. I want to be full of faith like Abraham, willing like Moses, courageous like Esther, a leader like Nehemiah, honest like Gideon, full of integrity like David, a father like Elijah, persistent like Elisha, devoted like Daniel, caring like Andrew, repentant like Peter, obsessed like John, transformed like Paul, and simply live entirely like Jesus.

Each of their lives has tremendous wealth for those who hear their testimony. Allow their stories to build your story. Everybody loves a good story, and hearing what Jesus has done is the best type of story available. However, this is a two-way street. As important as it is for you to tell your story to others, it is equally important for you to listen to the stories of others.

While pastoring at the church I grew up at, I remember calling several older people within the church and scheduling a time to meet with them for coffee. My intention was to simply listen to their stories. They told me tremendous stories about how they grew up and came to know the Lord. How they had remained faithful to God for decades. How they stayed married for so long. Miracles they had seen. Wars they fought in. I absolutely loved hearing what they had to say, and they loved sharing what they had experienced. Sometimes they would meet me at Starbucks, having brought with them pictures and trinkets that complimented their stories. They may or may not have known it at the time but they were inviting me into like experiences. I was listening full of faith and every seed they were sowing was landing on good soil.

I remember meeting with an elder in our church named Pastor David Torres. A man full of faith who came from a home built on faith. He shared with me the stories that had blessed him throughout his life. He told me about his dad who often experienced incredible supernatural circumstances. He once told me at Starbucks about a time his dad went with another person to go minister to a person at their home. While they were there, they were served something to drink, so they drank it. The host of the home disappeared for several minutes only to come back into the room baffled. "I don't understand why the both of you aren't dead! I poisoned your drinks and you should be long gone by now!" It was in that moment their attention was turned to the ceiling where a large black spot was forming. God had supernaturally taken the poison out of their drinks and put it on the ceiling! Needless to say, they now had the attention of this person and they were able to share the Gospel with her. Instead of her killing them, they led her to the Lord! After hearing this, I could have very simply said, "Cool story bro," and let that be it. Instead, I let it grow me. This one story has created such a confidence in me that the Lord will protect me through any danger the devil can throw at me. I still believe this way today and often think about that story whenever it applies to a dangerous circumstance I find myself in.

My nephew Clay was raised a Christian but his heart grew far from the Lord at a young age. He started hanging around the wrong crowd and got into drugs. After a while, not only was he doing them, he started dealing them as well. This went on for quite a while and his behavior in the house was increasingly rebellious. While he was acting belligerent, my family never stopped praying for him and reaching out to him. God was working on his heart behind the scenes of what we could see with our eyes. Long story short, my dad led his grandson, Clay, back to the Lord one night. It was amazing! As I spoke with my nephew he began telling me that if he was going to be a Christian, he was going to go all out. He would not tip-toe his way into this; he had to dive into the deep end. He didn't care if he lost his friends, or how radically his life would change. He knew he wanted God to have all of him. Hearing this coming from a senior in high school was extremely exciting!

A few days after his salvation, he called me late at night to ask my opinion on something. He told me that he had been dealing marijuana and knew he needed to stop, but he had recently "re-upped" and had over $2,000 worth of weed to sell. He needed some help getting rid of it in a safe way where nobody else would get it. I immediately drove to his house and together, along with my dad, we burned it all. (No, we didn't get high burning all that weed. We stood far enough away from it.) Clay told the Lord that night, "It took a lot of dedication and sacrifice to get all this product, but I was sacrificing all the wrong things like family time and relationship with those that love me. I had my priorities wrong. By destroying this, I make You my priority. I believe I can give up everything and know that You'll take care of me. I love You."

Today, Clay is on fire for God in the most remarkable way. He's praying for friends and family everywhere he goes. He's seeing God move miraculously in the lives of those close to him through healing when he prays for them. He's putting every penny he has into investing in his spiritual walk with God, and he's growing daily. As hard as he was running from the Lord for all those years, he's turned 180 degrees and is now running towards God with even greater fervor. Interestingly, it took him burning a great sacrifice to God in order for his life to become a sacrifice that God would then consume. Today he burns brighter, louder, and hotter than ever before!

These testimonies of what Jesus had done is prophesying to me and hopefully to you too. Consider finding somebody in your life, preferably somebody older with more experiences than you and simply ask them to tell you their story. While you are listening, pray in your spirit to the Lord saying this, "Do it again… Do It Again… DO IT AGAIN LORD!" Perhaps ask them to lay hands on you and pray for you to believe greater after hearing their stories. Let their testimonies impact you beyond entertainment.

18
Equally Yoked

I met my wife Ashley on February 20, 2009. I was so hungry for God that I always found myself going to gatherings wherever and whenever I could. She had just gotten out of a six-year-long relationship that she ended because her love for God was greater than that relationship, and she chose not to compromise. One night, out of her need to pray, she drove over thirty minutes to a conference, not to receive but to pour out to God in prayer. I happened to be at the same conference. At the end of the service after Benny Perez preached, there was a time of ministry to the people and I found myself pacing around the back of the room in prayer and worship. Ashley was on her face in the back of the room crying out to God. She wore a purple shirt, black pants, and purple heels. I passed by her several times as I prayed, not thinking much about her until I felt God put a prophetic word in my heart to share with her. I was nervous. Was I really hearing from the Lord? Was I just making something up so I could briefly talk with this girl? I argued with God for twenty minutes about delivering this word to her that I felt I heard. Finally, she picked herself up off the ground, said goodbye to a friend, and started making her way out of the building. My heart pounded in my chest as I said to myself, "If I don't tell her what I feel God told me to tell her, I'm so going to regret it!" So I chased her down through the church lobby and caught her just as she exited the building.

"Excuse me!" She stopped and turned around. "I'm sorry, I don't normally do this, but while I was praying in there I felt God gave me a word to share with you. Are you curious to know what it is?"

"Sure," she replied.

I proceeded to explain to her this word that I felt God had for her and little did I know how profound that word would be for her and how it would become a building block for our future relationship. It dealt with her identity as royalty, a princess—how God sees her. It was about balance coming into her life, with a strong significance on the number four. Where every corner of her life was coming into balance, amongst other things that the Father was communicating to His hurting daughter. I didn't know that she just found out some horrible stuff related to her ex and that particular day she was really hurting. God obviously knew that and was mending her heart as well as introducing her to her future spouse.

Little did I know that I wasn't just there to deliver this word to her, but I was part of the fulfillment of that prophetic promise to her. I often joke saying I told her, "I have a word from God for you…you will marry me! You will bear me a daughter who influence millions and change the earth! You will also give me an heir to my throne who will walk powerfully in the things of God! Go henceforth and fulfill your destiny!" That would have creeped her out and I probably would have gotten maced in the eyes.

After I shared with her what God had actually told me, she received it gladly and we chatted for a minute or two and then I invited her to a conference that my church was hosting the following day. I figured, if she enjoyed the conference we were just at, she would love this one too, so we exchanged numbers. Slick, right?

She did not come to that conference, and for about a week, I texted her several times to which she would rarely respond. Occasionally she would text back hours later. She was sending every indication that she was not interested in talking with me. Why would she? Knowing what I know now, she was protecting her relationship with God. She just left a long relationship for the Lord; looking for another relationship was nowhere near her radar. She was laser-focused on God and God alone.

Now, both of us prior to meeting each other had made a commitment to the Lord that we were not going to jump into any relationships without God guiding us. We were both done dating just to date; we were both willing to seek God first and allow Him to bring our spouse when the timing was right. I had dated around a lot, and all of which was not the right relationship to be in. God didn't initiate them, I did. I was hunting for the one instead of pursuing Him passionately and allowing Him to bring her to me.

I remember walking into work as a valet one week after I had met Ashley and I told the Lord, "I feel like I'm bugging her and I don't want to do that, so I'm gonna send her one more text, and if she doesn't respond, I'll let her go. If she does respond, awesome! But I don't want to be annoying." I texted her, and she responded! We talked my whole 8-hour shift, and from that point forward our relationship began to build. We were just friends at first, as any healthy relationship should start. Almost a month later we knew we had feelings for each other but we wanted to be sure that God was in this. So we both decided to separately fast at the same time in order to get confirmation from God.

During our fast, we were not speaking to each other and Ashley was listening to a sermon on the radio where the preacher quoted a Scripture that stood out to her. She wrote that Scripture down as she felt the Lord was speaking to her through it. At the same time, I was on a 3-day fast—no food, no water, and on the third day feeling physically depleted, I felt like the Lord brought a verse to my mind that was so out of the blue it had to be God, so I wrote it down. At the end of the fast, just before Ashley and

I were going to talk with each other, we both emailed each other at the same time so as not to manipulate each other with what we felt we heard from God and then called each other right away. We were blown away to discover that out of all the verses in the Bible, the Lord had spoken to us separately the very same verse as confirmation for us to move forward! It was unbelievable.

"A man's heart plans his way,
But the LORD directs his steps" (Prov. 16:9
NKJV).

We knew that we were planning our way, but God was ultimately directing our steps. He was in control. Even though what He was doing didn't make sense in many ways, He knew what He was doing. I can't find the Scripture that says, "God has given us common sense." Though I agree that common sense is a good thing and certainly proves helpful, it is not the basis for every decision we should make. Common sense would not drive Noah to build an ark in the middle of the wilderness when it had never rained before. Common sense would not put a young shepherd boy up against a giant when the lives of thousands were at stake. Common sense would not whittle an army down to 300 in order to take on thousands. Common sense would not choose ordinary, untrained, everyday men to change the world. Sometimes what the Lord is doing makes perfect sense and sometimes it makes no sense at all. The only safe bet is to trust in Him in every situation no matter how safe or risky it appears.

There were countless more confirmations of how equally yoked Ashley and I were after we started dating on April 16, 2009. Time and time again we would laugh together at how God was framing our lives together so perfectly.

We learned a lot about what it meant to be equally

yoked during this time. Equally yoked was not a matter of ensuring we were both Christians; equally yoked was a matter of pace. When two oxen were yoked together for the purpose of tilling the soil, it was imperative that the team of oxen were trained to walk together at the same pace. They had to be equally yoked. If one ox were more ambitious than the other, the entire mechanism would turn sideways and topple over, or at the very least, not till a straight line. If you were a farmer, having equally yoked oxen was invaluable. Paul's encouragement to the Corinthian church was: **"Do not be unequally yoked together with unbelievers. For what fellowship has righteousness with lawlessness? And what communion has light with darkness?" (2 Cor. 6:14 NKJV).**

How much more does this apply when yoking up with your spouse? Since being equally yoked is a matter of pace, those looking for their spouse should run as fast as they can after King Jesus with everything in them and then see who around them is keeping up with their pace. Who is consecrating themselves to the lifestyle of prayer that they are? Who is abandoning themselves to the things of God like they are? Who is forsaking all other lovers to devote themselves entirely to the Lord like they are? The ones that are keeping up with your pace are the legitimate prospects for marriage.

Please don't settle for somebody who calls themselves a Christian, goes to church, but really doesn't have any thriving relationship with God. Our job is to **"...seek first the kingdom of God and His righteousness, and all these things shall be added to you" (Matt. 6:33 NKJV).** Yoking yourself up with somebody who will slow your pace can be disastrous. Seek His Kingdom at full throttle and only consider those who are doing the same.

Simply run after Him. He will take care of bringing

you your spouse when you have reached your top speed. Then when your spouse does come, that individual will only fuel your fire to run even faster. My dad always prayed for me to find a woman who loved the Lord more than I did. My prideful self said, "Sure dad, who is out there that loves the Lord more than I do?" Sure enough, Ashley was precisely that for me. Her honest, simple, passionate, black and white, relentless love for the Lord took my faith to another level. I may have had more Biblical understanding than she did, but her love for God was so clear and concise that it wiped away how cloudy my love for God had become. I felt like I was falling in love with Him all over again as I was falling in love with her.

This is how your spouse should encourage your relationship with the Lord. That person should encourage your love for God. Their number one priority in all the world should be to see your walk with God burn brighter, louder, longer, and hotter than ever before. When that happens, your love for that equally yoked person will grow as a secondary consequence. If you are already married and your spouse is not doing this for you right now, begin to model it first and foremost. Invest in their relationship with the Lord and begin to pray. Never underestimate what God can do for your marriage through your passionate prayers. If you feel stuck, start seeking God unlike never before. Host His presence within your home well. Start praying and worshipping unlike never before. Ask God to start shifting your spouse's heart in ways that nobody else possibly could. What have you got to lose?

On February 20, 2010, one year after the day we met, to the day, I'd planned on proposing to Ashley. Up until this point, Ashley had been asking God for more and more confirmations concerning us getting married. God had already given us dozens and dozens of them but she wanted more. It was fun watching God confirm what He had planned for us. If you're seeking confirmations from the Lord for something, buckle up because it's an exciting ride watching Him direct and confirm your life.

The engagement ring was tied to a ribbon inside her Bible at John chapter 13 along with four flower pedals on the page to represent our special significant number. We were driving to sunset cliffs and when I merged onto the I-15 freeway, I noticed a car right in front of us had written on their license plate, "Psalms 48". Without thinking, I said, "Hey look, Psalms 48!" To which Ashley replied, "Let's read it." Then she reached for her Bible which had the ring in it. She started thumbing through the pages, searching for Psalms 48 as I was practically sweating bullets while driving the car. I tried to distract her by telling her to use my version of the Bible and handed her my Bible to which she stubbornly said, "No, I don't want to read *your* version!"

She read through Psalms 48, and honestly, I couldn't pay attention to anything she was saying because I was trying to quickly come up with a plan B in case she discovered the ring. Should I pull over on the side of the freeway and romantically drop to my knee asking her to marry me? No photographer. No secret video. No feet washing at the beach at sunset. This was not what I had in mind.

When she got to the last verse of Psalms 48, it struck her deeply.

> **For this *is* God,**
> **Our God forever and ever;**
> **He will be our guide**
> ***Even* to death (Psa. 48:14 NKJV).**

It hit her then but didn't hit me until later, that once again, God was using this Scripture to confirm that He was guiding what we were doing unto death do us part. Our relationship started with Him guiding our steps, and it will be sustained by Him guiding our steps. Every other person out there should expect nothing less from their marital relationship. This is why it is so crucial to keep God at the center of all that happens in our lives in order to ensure that He remains a guide we can trust with everything in us. When it makes sense and when it doesn't make sense. Seek first His Kingdom, search for Him, and only even consider those truly equally yoked that He brings across your path as a future spouse and watch how He will guide you.

On August 20, 2010…six months after we got engaged, we were married. He had truly guided our path from day one and still guides our path today. Everything began on a word from God and now our day-to-day is sustained by the word of the Lord. Sometimes we have lots of money in the bank and sometimes we're scraping by, trusting Him every step of the way, but it never shakes our faith. Sometimes it's smooth sailing, and sometimes we feel we're in the eye of the storm, but our faith in Him always encourages us. Ecclesiastes 4:9-10 NLT states that **"two people are better off than one, for they can help each other succeed. If one person falls, the other can reach out and help. But someone who falls alone is in real trouble."**

Troubles sure do come. Mistakes happen. There will be countless opportunities to render justice or dispense grace. However, when you are grounded in Him, nothing shakes that faith in Him. We know Who our guide is. We rely on His Spirit to provide every single thing we have need of. We can do this with confidence because Ashley and I both remember all that God did to confirm that we were meant to be together. So if we have a bad day, there is never once a thought that says, "Maybe this isn't right…" Those are lies from the enemy, and we can clearly see that because we are absolutely one hundred percent convinced this relationship is equally yoked and of God.

If you're currently married but your pace is not equal with your spouse, evaluate who is moving faster and develop a plan to get the other to keep up. Find times to pray together. Read the Word together. Have times of worship before bed. Journal together. Go to a conference together. Hold hands during worship. Start investing in your spiritual relationship with the Lord, together. If your spouse is unwilling to do anything then it's time to start praying and hosting the presence of God within your home. The Lord will do what you can't, but you should do what you can. You can pray. You can worship. You can intercede. If you're not married than do everything you can to ensure your potential marriage relationship is equally yoked. It is well worth the wait and the fight.

19
Preparations

The day and age we live in wants results quickly and efficiently with the least amount of effort as possible. When I was in high school, I always found myself cutting corners. I was trying to skate my way through to graduation by doing the least amount of work as possible. I wasn't putting any effort to get A's, but I was a smart kid and wasn't failing any classes. Just mediocre. Average. I knew that school was preparing me for the "real world—adult life" but I wasn't taking it very seriously.

I am discovering that so many people treat their faith in God the same way. Little to no preparations for what God has in store for them. They wait for the next pitch and try to figure out how to swing the bat as the pitch is coming. With little to no spiritual batting practice, nobody is ready for what God throws their way and we constantly strikeout.

As a pastor, I know that my heart is to help prepare those God has given me stewardship over to be ready for the next pitch. To be ready for what God has in store for their lives. To prepare them for their destiny. The frustrating truth I find is that so many don't want to be prepared. They want mind-blowing encounters with God but they don't ready themselves, their homes, their schedules, or their priorities to receive these encounters. They want to step into full-time ministry but they don't ready themselves academically for what the future holds. Even more importantly, they don't ready themselves spiritually for what lies ahead. You can't expect to hit homers while constantly skipping batting practice. I know several people in full-time ministry that are advanced academically but have incredibly poor relationships with God. They are so busy doing things for Him, that they don't do much of anything with Him. He is their boss and not their Father. Somebody, somewhere in their past, did not prepare them properly. This breaks my heart. Perhaps they were prepared for some things that matter, but certainly not the most important thing that matters.

Preparations often take a long time and can be a grueling process. Depending on what you are being prepared for may determine how long it takes and how intense the preparations are. It is no secret how much effort and time goes into an Olympic athlete's moment of competition. What they are competing for is history in the making or pride for themselves or their nation. It's no wonder the preparations are so intense. The prize is equal to the sacrifice.

I remember crying out to God for some pretty radical things. I wanted a lasting revival to sweep across my city. For San Diego to become a hub for the presence of God, where people would travel here from all over the world to be in His presence. I wanted the churches to unite unlike never before. I wanted our petty differences to fall by the way-side and for His glory in our midst to become our only satisfaction. I wanted an awakening to break into our military and for that awakening to spread like wild-fire all over the world as our military was sent on missions all around the world. Ordered and paid for by the government, a revival would begin spreading globally through the American military. I didn't know what exactly my place was in all this, but I simply wanted to be involved. I knew that I was asking for a lot. One day, the Lord told me while thinking on all this, "Josiah, your measure of sacrifice determines your level of anointing." I was asking God for involvement in some pretty incredible things. I wanted a radical anointing to accompany these powerful prayers, but

I was sacrificing very little. I didn't want to be inconvenienced. I didn't want anything to really change in my life. How could I be so silly? I would have to sacrifice far more if I wanted the things I was believing for to come to pass. I needed to start preparing myself.

I recently received a message from somebody looking to give away their pool table. Typically, when I receive a message like this I'm not too interested because most people are just giving away not great condition items but something led me to probe a little further. I called and asked about the condition of the table, and the gentlemen giving it away said that I would be more than pleased with the condition and I had to come see it. We were at the drive-thru for In-n-Out Burger at the moment (which is where Jesus eats by the way), and we had some free time so we went straight to his house.

When I laid eyes on the table for the first time, I had a flash back to my childhood, playing pool on my dad's pool table in our garage when I lived with my parents. I remember mentioning years ago that if I ever got a pool table I would want a red felt table with black sides. I thought it would be different and look cool. Sure enough, this table was red felt with black sides and was in perfect condition! I couldn't believe my eyes. I felt that God was romancing me in that moment. He then showed us the great bonus, there was a heavy-duty, official ping-pong table top that fits on top of the table as well. I think I love ping-pong even more than pool so this was the cherry on top for sure.

The table came with everything it needed: cues, a cue rack, the balls, chalk, 8 ball rack, 9-ball rack, EVERYTHING…for free. There was one problem. I didn't have a place to put the table…yet. I knew it would fit in my garage but our garage was a disaster. We hadn't cleaned it since we moved into the house we were staying at. When I got home, we got to work on cleaning out the garage. Throwing away junk and clutter that had been there for years. I was preparing myself to receive the blessing of this pool table.

It didn't take long before the Holy Spirit began to speak to me about the lesson He was trying to show me. I had to clean out all the things that I had kept, all the junk, all the clutter that I didn't want to let go of, in order to receive this greater blessing. That's exactly what God is always trying to do with each one of us. We are holding on to so many things that clutter our minds and hearts and we have no room to receive what God wants to bless us with spiritually because there is no room to receive it. It is silly to hold onto a box of clothes that no longer fit, baby items that we no longer use, and household items that are either broken or unusable, when those things will hinder a far greater blessing. We have to let these things go.

I wonder what we are holding onto that is keeping us from receiving the blessings He has for us. I wonder what unforgiveness is stashed away in the garages of our hearts that is keeping us from receiving His forgiveness today? What resentment do we have toward the church or a pastor that was a spiritual authority to us that's currently keeping us from the great things He has for reserved with our name on it? I'm convinced He wants to bless us, but we have to clean out the clutter. We have to prepare ourselves for the greater blessing. It's possible that somebody reading this had an incident, or a memory come to their mind simply by reading those last few sentences. That may be the Holy Spirit bringing up some clutter so you could be rid of it. Please stop sweeping it under the rug. Don't look away. Invite the grace of God to help you in this. His grace is staring down that monster of unforgiveness or hurt and empowering you to deal with it. Give it a try, you may be pleasantly surprised.

It took me three days to clean out the garage. It was a lot of time and effort but once I set up my pool table and played my first game it was well worth it. The preparations paid off.

Jesus knew that a day was coming when He was going to leave His disciples here on earth, and He was going to a place they could not follow. So He prepared them for that moment many times by telling them about it beforehand. He also made it abundantly clear that He was not abandoning them; in fact, He had prepared a way for God to be with them always through the presence of the Holy Spirit. All they had to do was be obedient to what Jesus was instructing them to do and they would be ready. He thoroughly prepared them for success.

Here we are today, still impacted by the preparations Jesus made two thousand years ago. Do yourself a favor, don't cut corners. There is a process that cannot be sped-up faster than His timing will allow. Submit to the preparations needed to be ready for all He has for you. Clean out the clutter and receive the blessing.

The great "prophet," Queen Elsa, from Disney's *Frozen,* once sang, "Let it go!" Instead of concealing her magical ice powers, she found a way to let it go and release the power she had. This restored her relationship with her sister and ultimately saved the kingdom. Now she was free to reign without having to hide the power within. But first, she had to let it go and let nothing hold her back anymore. A blessing awaited her, but she had to first let it go.

Prepare yourself for the blessings awaiting you…and maybe consider watching Frozen. For me, it would be the millionth time!

20
SPIRITUALLY KNOWN

We give a lot of attention to our reputations in the natural world, but I wonder what our spiritual reputations are like. We certainly do live in a spiritual world, and I have always believed that the spiritual world we live in is as real—or even more real—than the physical world we know so well.

In the culture I live in, your reputation is a big deal. Everybody is trying to get more followers or friends on social media. Everybody wants other people to know what they are doing. Everybody is seeking fame and fortune. Social status seems to be at the top of most people's priority list or at least pretty close to it.

If we put a fraction of the effort and attention we put into our natural reputations into our spiritual reputations, we might just become a force to be reckoned with. I believe there needs to be a shift in the mindset of believers today, especially in America. The caring so much about our natural reputation needs to shift into an acceleration and recognition of our spiritual reputation.

When we are aware of the spiritual world we live in, a secondary consequence of that revelation is the realization that we are really nothing without Christ. So, an appropriate posture of thankfulness and praise is offered to God because there's an understanding that we're only anything great because He is great. His love for us and His redemption of our souls by His precious blood is the only reason we can have any good spiritual reputation. Otherwise we'll get trampled by demonic powers over and over again. I say this to be clear, when I refer to our spiritual reputation, it is out of a humble spirit that recognizes He has done it all! His work in my life is why I can have any positive spiritual reputation at all. This is not acquired by my gifting or hard work. It all starts with what He's done for me.

We need to begin to see people through God's eyes, recognizing their spiritual caliber. In most of the churches I see, the value placed upon people is based upon their natural gifting. Their skills, personality, availability, desire to attribute to the church in the many areas of need. Little value seems to be placed upon the spiritual caliber of those within the church. I would like to submit to you that this is backward. Though the natural talents and gifting of individuals is highly crucial to the church and a necessary contribution we should all prayerfully consider and be active in. Still, I believe the spiritual contribution is far greater.

I have personally served in so many capacities within the church. You name it, I've probably done it. Apart from singing...I reserve that for my poor family; pray for them. My servant's heart will never cease. I believe we are called of God to do so, but I know that my sweet spot is to invest into the spiritual health of the church.

I was talking to a friend earlier today who recently suffered a shoulder injury and has been in recovery. This guy has demonstrated a servant's heart as long as I have known him. In many scenarios when nobody else was available to help, he was there. His dedication is obvious and an enduring example. While recruiting the help for an event coming up, he mentioned he couldn't help because of his injury, and so I felt led to remind him that what he can contribute spiritually is perhaps far greater than the physical service he can provide. Both are needed, but he has always been more of a benefit to the spiritual atmosphere than the natural. I already know his heart is to help in the natural, that's a given and he's proven it time and again, but spiritually I see something greater in him that can be developed.

I hesitate to offer any opportunity to the person who wants a spiritual platform to minister and will not help in the natural needs of the church. But I jump on the opportunity to create a platform for the person who wants to minister spiritually and has proved their willingness to serve the natural needs as well. There is something about faithfulness in the natural that creates a platform for you in the spiritual. It's a process. One most people don't want to take. Many would prefer to cut corners, rely on their gifting and personality to shoot straight to the most prestigious position desired without building their Kingdom reputation first.

There was nothing about Jesus' physical appearance that communicated He was the Messiah. He didn't show up with a six pack, perfect tan, long, flowing, beautiful hair, with pearly white teeth and radiating eyes. **"My servant grew up in the LORD's presence like a tender green shoot, like a root in dry ground. There was nothing beautiful or majestic about His appearance, nothing to attract us to Him" (Isa. 53:2 NLT).**

Could you imagine being near Jesus but not recognizing that He was indeed the very Son of God? He passed by so many people who never knew that He was God in the flesh, walking amongst them. What an incredible privilege to even be alive during the time that He walked the earth and to miss that revelation is an unfathomable waste.

This story communicates the importance of being spiritually known well:

> **When he came to the village of Nazareth, his boyhood home, he went as usual to the synagogue on the Sabbath and stood up to read the Scriptures. The scroll of**

Isaiah the prophet was handed to him. He unrolled the scroll and found the place where this was written:

> **"The Spirit of the LORD is upon me, for he has anointed me to bring Good News to the poor. He has sent me to proclaim that captives will be released, that the blind will see, that the oppressed will be set free, and that the time of the LORD's favor has come."**

He rolled up the scroll, handed it back to the attendant, and sat down. All eyes in the synagogue looked at him intently. Then he began to speak to them. "The Scripture you've just heard has been fulfilled this very day! (Luke 4:16-21 NLT)

Something remarkable happened in this moment. The long awaited coming of the Messiah was over. The Anointed One Himself was publicly declaring the fulfillment of Isaiah's famous prophecy concerning the manifestation of the Messiah. The people within the synagogue that day would have certainly been familiar with this passage. They had probably heard it read dozens of times, or likely committed it to memory, but this time something was different. This time there was an authority, an ownership of the words within the prophecy. Not simply reading it for what it says, but reading it as a declaration of reality. Something beautiful was surely happening. I bet it felt like the air was sucked out of the room when Jesus read the passage and then sat down. They probably could hear a pin drop…jaws were on the floor…people wide eyed, gazing at the proclaimed Messiah.

"Everyone spoke well of him and was amazed by the gracious words that came from his lips. 'How can this be?' they asked. 'Isn't this Joseph's son?'" (Luke 4:22 NLT).

The people noticed the grace saturating what He was declaring from His lips but then doubt came rushing into the room. "Isn't this Joseph's son?" This can't be the Messiah He's claiming to be; we watched Him grow up. We saw Him down the street playing after school. We saw Him on the baseball team like every other kid. We know His family.

What they understood of Jesus was the natural things that were all too familiar to them. Unfortunately, they were about to pay an extremely steep price for not recognizing Him according to the spiritual. Can you imagine deciding to go to church this day, and that happens to be the day that Jesus declares Himself the Messiah that everybody had been waiting on for thousands of years! Imagine what it was like to be there when that moment came. When it happened, your heart sunk into your stomach, you broke out into a cold sweat, a nervous chill ran down your spine, a rush of excitement filled your body like thousands of volts of electricity, but then somebody from the back of the room casts a seed of doubt. "Nah, ignore everything we think we're feeling right now, it couldn't be, this is Jesus...we all know Him."

If those gathered there that day would have been able to discern the spiritual in that moment, they would have recognized that this was no ordinary moment and Jesus was no ordinary man. They would have sensed God on Him. They would have sensed the significance of the moment. But instead they only saw Him with natural eyes, and nothing about His natural appearance was communicating that He was indeed God. So the people missed it.

There is a terribly steep price to pay for not knowing people according to their spiritual counterpart. The same remains true today. We are constantly surrounded by the spiritual world, but we fail to recognize people's spiritual caliber because they are the same kids who grew up in our youth group. They're the same praying grandmas who have been attending your church for decades. They're the same pastors you've heard preach a thousand times and then grabbed a burger with after service. It's the same friend, same building, same city, same preacher, same singer you're all too familiar with…so they couldn't be the answer you're waiting for. Right?

I wonder how many people are currently in our lives right now that are spiritual giants in the Kingdom of God. Heaven and hell know them, but we haven't given them the time of day because we don't think they carry much spiritual significance at all. When we pray for breakthrough we think it will come by the guest speaker, or conference host, lead pastor, or some other prestigious individual. Though it certainly can, I know the spiritual weight resting on those perhaps sitting right next to us are equally as powerful. Oh, what a steep price we will pay for failing to see them for who they really are.

Have you ever heard the phrase, "God's man of power for the hour"? I remember it mentioned a lot in the 90's. Traveling evangelists would come through the city and churches would be packed out hoping to have him/her pray for them. *If I could just get the mighty man of God to lay hands on me my problems will be solved.* This created job security for those traveling around because they were apparently the only ones God was really doing any significant things through. They seemingly had a monopoly on the power of God.

As years went by, there began to be a shift in the church culture. It was no longer about that one mighty man but about training everybody to also walk in the power of God. The revelation that the spiritual leaders didn't get some massive dosage of Holy Spirit and everybody else got a clearance rack version of Him changed everything. The school teacher, construction worker, student, mom, banker, CEO, computer tech could do the things Jesus said they could do as well. When this shift started to happen, I'm sure that some who made their living by itinerant speaking were concerned about their jobs, but they would soon discover that there was indeed a greater job security in equipping the saints for the work of ministry compared to what they had been doing. Not to mention it was the heart of the Father.

I remember seeing ministers spend hours walking through the crowd laying hands on thousands of people late into the night. Exhausted, they would steward the call of God on their lives the best they could. Now there's a better way. Now the spiritual reputation of the everyday believer can be equipped and anointed to do the very same things. Ask any itinerant speaker and they would probably agree that they have seen far more breakthroughs, far more miracles, far more divine intervention through the body ministering to the body than by their own personal interaction.

Without giving too many details or spoiling the movie if you haven't seen it, in the most recently released Star Wars movie, *The Last Jedi*, an unprecedented shift occurred. The force was no longer a power that only the Jedi possessed. It was something that everybody had access to if they knew how to tap into it. It's not that nobody was special anymore, it's that more and more people were remarkable now. A similar thing has happened in the Church and thank God it has. The force is strong with us.

The spiritual gift: discerning of spirits, is not just discerning when angels and demons are around and what they are doing, like I used to think. It is essentially discerning the spiritual. It is recognizing the spiritual fingerprints on everything around us. Considering our context, it is measuring the degree of spiritual caliber upon the people God has placed within our lives. Such a helpful gift when we consider how many individuals sit week after week in our churches that are spiritually radical and passionate about the things of God, but because they are introverts we overlook them. Perhaps they don't dress the way we would expect a mighty man of God or woman of God should dress. Perhaps they don't act, talk, walk, socialize, or preach like the others we've known in the past worthy enough to place spiritual value upon.

That has to change. We have got to begin to recognize the spiritual caliber of the people who are already within our lives. These are the types of people we should consider yoking ourselves together with. I have friends who carry a lot of God in them, but if it wasn't for their passionate relationships with the Lord, I probably wouldn't really be friends with them. Simply because we don't have much else in common. But I have begun to recognize who they are spiritually, and consequently I make great effort to yoke myself to them. I have discovered that a wonderful way to grow in my relationship with the Lord is to surround myself with people who will help boost my faith to the next level simply by allowing their spiritual person to rub shoulders with my own. To simplify, when you hang around people who carry a lot of God on them, they rub off on you and so does He.

Paul said, "**So we have stopped evaluating others from a human point of view. At one time we thought of Christ merely from a human point of view. How differently we know him now!" (2 Cor. 5:16 NLT).**

Once the people who knew Jesus as a mere Man recognized that He was indeed God, their perspective shifted concerning everybody else in their life. I am sure they were wondering, "What secrets do you have? What kind of spiritually radical tricks do you have up your sleeves?" If we only evaluate people from a human point of view, we are missing the most important dimension of an individual's life. To further this thought, just look at the next verse**: "This means that anyone who belongs to Christ has become a new person. The old life is gone; a new life has begun!" (2 Cor. 5:17 NLT).**

The person who evaluates Jesus according to His natural self and misses His spiritual reality makes a *huge* mistake. The person who evaluates a born-again believer only according to their natural self and overlooks their spiritual counterpart is also making a huge mistake. Paul made it clear, "The old life is gone; a new life has begun!" If this is true, then some drastic changes should be evident in the life of a newborn believer. The old should be passing away and the new life beginning. This obvious transformation is naturally complimented by the clear spiritual transformation. A spiritual new-creation is birthed at the point of salvation; that's a pretty noteworthy change. As far as I can tell, Christians are the first newly created anything on the planet since Genesis chapter 1. I don't know about you, but that makes me feel pretty special.

There is a wonderful story about the importance of seeing someone spiritually that is found in 2 Kings. Elisha is following Elijah, awaiting his mantle to be passed onto him. He had requested that a double portion of the spirit that

180

was upon Elijah come upon him. Long story short, the moment finally came where Elijah was taken up in a whirlwind to Heaven and the mantle of Elijah fell to Elisha. He took it, and sure enough the power that was upon Elijah now rested with Elisha. He struck the Jordan river and the river split for Elisha to walk across on dry ground.

Now, catch this: **"When the group of prophets from Jericho saw from a distance what happened, they exclaimed, "Elijah's spirit rests upon Elisha!" And they went to meet him and bowed to the ground before him"** **(2 Kings 2:15 NLT).**

Their response was good thus far.

> **"Sir," they said, "just say the word and fifty of our strongest men will search the wilderness for your master. Perhaps the Spirit of the LORD has left him on some mountain or in some valley."**
> **"No," Elisha said, "don't send them."**
> **But they kept urging him until they shamed him into agreeing, and he finally said, "All right, send them." So fifty men searched for three days but did not find Elijah.**
> **Elisha was still at Jericho when they returned. "Didn't I tell you not to go?" he asked. (2 Kings 2:16-18 NLT)**

At first, it appears that they recognize the spirit that is upon Elisha, but apparently not entirely. I believe they still had a hard time getting past the fact that this was Elisha. Someone they knew, someone they were familiar with. They didn't have spiritual eyes to see the double portion that now rested upon him. If they had eyes to see the double portion standing right in front of them, they wouldn't have cared much at all to go back and look for Elijah, who, at that moment, was only half the anointing Elisha was carrying.

It is pointless to abandon double to go look for half simply because half is familiar and double is not. Rest assured, God is doing a new thing. That new thing the Lord may be doing in your church, city, or family may be double compared to what He has done in the past, but be careful not to miss it because it comes unfamiliar to you. The music of double may be different than the music of half, and it may be unfamiliar to you but that doesn't mean it is not what God is doing. The lights may look unfamiliar, the preaching may be unfamiliar, the demands of God inciting obedience may be unfamiliar, but if it is God, you can bet it's beneficial. It may be what the church was doing 40 years ago, but if there's a fresh wind on it, because it's what God is saying to do now, then that may be the double for that moment.

I've never been much into hymns. No church I've ever been a part of ever really sang them very often. I have nothing against them, but hymns are just not my particular favorite style of worship music. But if there is a fresh wind on hymns and God speaks to us to start singing them in our modern-day services because there is a double portion available for us when we are obedient to start singing those hymns again, you'd better believe I'm going to start singing them! I want His manifest presence far more than my favorite style. I want to recognize what is happening spiritually and respond accordingly. That is what these men failed to recognize in Elisha walking in his new spiritual caliber. So, they wasted three days looking for a lesser thing when what God was clearly doing in that moment was standing right in front of them.

Pastor Bill Johnson from Bethel Church tells a story about a man who is walking through the airport with his wife. They stop and put their bags down; he tells his wife,

"Watch the bags. I'll be right back." He backtracks himself and finds a man standing amidst the crowd. His wife watches from a distance as he hugs this man, gives him a kiss on the cheek, talks with him for a moment, and then leaves him.

Upon returning she asks him, "Who was that?"

He replies, "I have no idea, but I smelled a fragrance on him that I've only ever smelled in the throne room of God…so I knew he had to be a powerful man of prayer."

He recognized what this person was spiritually carrying in the place of prayer, and went out of his way to honor him and thank him for being a man of prayer. This guy looked so unassuming to so many others, but spiritually he was a giant. Makes me wonder, what do I smell like? Spiritually, that is!

A couple months ago I was talking with a friend of mine whose dedication to the Lord and His Kingdom is second to none. He is amazing! We were going to pray for something and the moment I grabbed his hand, a rush of the presence of the Holy Spirit came over me and brought me to tears. It happened the very moment I touched him; I could feel that tangible spiritual anointing he carries. I'm learning to pay attention to the spiritual climate of those I interact with. By noticing, I'm also honoring. By honoring, I'm inviting. By inviting, I'm transforming.

Now, I'm convinced that we have a spiritual counterpart to our lives. But most people don't know us by this spiritual reality of ourselves, we only know each other after this physical realm. The way we see each other now. That's like seeing somebody and thinking you know them but having never actually had a conversation with them. There's far more to them than appearances alone.

I want to develop a strong spiritual reputation. I want to be known in Heaven and hell. I want Heaven to desire to partner with me concerning the will of God on the earth, and I want hell to fear me, not because I'm anything great, but because I carry a radical authority and am not afraid to use it. I am a son of the Most High God. I know I am called to plunder hell for a living. If Jesus came to destroy the works of the devil, I should consider my destiny one in the same.

Here is one final story relating to being known spiritually:

"God gave Paul the power to perform unusual miracles. When handkerchiefs or aprons that had merely touched his skin were placed on sick people, they were healed of their diseases, and evil spirits were expelled" **(Acts 19:11-12 NLT).**

That's just cool. Keep it in mind.

Acts 19:13-15 NLT states that **"A group of Jews was traveling from town to town casting out evil spirits. They tried to use the name of the Lord Jesus in their incantation, saying, 'I command you in the name of Jesus, whom Paul preaches, to come out!'**

Seven sons of Sceva and a leading priest were doing this.

But one time when they tried it, the evil spirit replied, 'I know Jesus, and I know Paul, but who are you?'"

Uh oh. These guys thought there was some secret incantation they could recite in order to make the devils respond to them. Well, they do get a response but it is not what they were hoping for. The demons actually beat them up, stripped them naked, and chased them away. But I love that the evil spirits mentioned that they knew Jesus and they knew Paul. Jesus and Paul both had a spiritual reputation. These other guys were maybe well intended, but had too weak a spiritual maturity to get the job done. Their spiritual reputation was non-existent, hence their failure.

Several years ago I was eating with Ashley at a California Pizza Kitchen near our home. I noticed somebody walk in and start talking to the manager at the front and this guy sort of looked like LaDainian Tomlinson, the San Diego Chargers running back at the time. I told Ashley that LT just walked in, and she looked over her shoulder at him. "Is that seriously LT?"

"Yup, that's him!" I replied. We kept looking over at him, somewhat snickering, and he even looked back at us with a strange complexion on his face as he then started walking with the manager back behind the counter to the kitchen of the restaurant.

"What's he doing here?" She asked me.

"Oh, he owns several CPK's throughout the west coast." I lied.

We finished our meal, paid and then left.

The next day a buddy of mine working as a valet told me that his girlfriend who works at CPK saw me in there yesterday. He went on to tell me that the store was being robbed at the moment that we were in the restaurant! He said that right after we left the cops showed up and the whole place turned into a crime scene. The robber told the manager some personal information and made him open the safe for him, otherwise bad things would happen to his family, so the manager complied. The LT look-alike was robbing the place, and we didn't have a clue. If we would have been paying attention to the spiritual atmosphere we may have had some discernment about what was happening and acted differently. I now think back on the situation and am grateful to God for His protection over us, and I also kick myself in the tail for being so spiritually blind.

I am learning to build my understanding of what is happening spiritually around me at all times. The more I am aware of what's going on, the more I am able to partner with the Holy Spirit and see His purposes come to fruition in the world around me.

Does Heaven know your name? Do angels hearken to your command because you're walking in such a closeness to the Lord that you begin to partner with Almighty God in order to see His will accomplished on the earth? Does hell know you exist? Or do you pose so little a threat to the kingdom of darkness that they don't even pay attention to you? We should be known spiritually. The spiritual world should know who we are and Who we carry inside of us. We should also be aware of the spiritual world around us. If it's true that we are building a strong spiritual reputation, I think it is very important that we begin to not only recognize that spiritual caliber upon ourselves but also upon individuals around us. We need to honor what they carry in the spirit. We should yoke ourselves to them. We have to pray and ask the Holy Spirit to lead and guide our steps and our relationships to those whose spiritual counterparts can encourage our own to glorify the King in all that we do.

21
THE AMERICAN CHURCH

I feel compelled to share some things on my heart concerning the American church. I have talked a lot about some bad habits that we as Americans within the church have developed. We are often driven by entertainment, self-centeredness, spiritual laziness, complacency, immaturity, and several other sad truths. That being said, I know that the devil never goes to war where there are no spoils. I believe the enemy sees the potential of the American church far more clearly than most American Christians do. If she wakes up and becomes the spiritual giant she's destined to be, the world will never be the same. America has experienced some incredible moves of God in recent years, and she is poised for an awakening that will never fade away.

I love the fact that my country was founded on God-honoring principles. Almighty God was on the minds and hearts of many of our founding fathers and for this reason, I believe America has been phenomenally blessed. As a nation, are we without sin? Absolutely not. Have we participated in incredible offenses in the eyes of God? Guilty as charged. Have we passed laws that justified our actions and only further distanced us from righteousness? Fact. Still, like a prodigal nation, it's not too late to turn our hearts back to the God of this nation, enabling Him to put a robe on her back, sandals on her feet, a signet ring on her finger, and see her become all He's dreamt for her to be.

A move of God on a national scale like this sounds unfathomable, doesn't it? As I have driven from state to state, I've often thought how impossible it seems to reach all these people. There are just so many. I know it won't happen through stadiums and arenas being filled, although that may be part of it. I know it won't happen by getting the right person in the oval office, though we should vote according to Biblical conviction as much as possible. I know it won't happen by building bigger churches and filling them, though I'm all about growing churches. I believe the answer is found in those who already know Jesus Christ as Lord and Savior, fueling the fire that burns within them and being so led of the Spirit that they do what Jesus did. If we forsook every other lover and made our obsession all things King Jesus, our flames would never dwindle. If those already attending churches in my city were to really get this, we'd turn the city upside. Souls would get saved daily. Discipleship would be as normal as breathing. Righteousness would abound. Miracles would put a grand spot light on Jesus, not the persons praying for them to be done. The attention of the nation and even the world would be on my city. When people discover that this was not some model our city would package and sell but a repentance into a lifestyle transformation, they could begin starting fires in their own cities. Perhaps, one by one, city by city, state by state…this nation would burn for the King unlike never before.

America has been given much, therefore much will be required of her. She's already been a blessing to the world in ways I can't even comprehend nor articulate. But I believe her greatest gift to the world is yet to be given. I believe she is yet to show the world a non-hypocritical, unified, full of power, Christian nation. The best is certainly yet to come. I don't believe that the judgment of God is going to fall on this nation so Jesus can come remove His Church from the planet and we'll all dance on streets of gold in the morning. America is not going to hell in a hand-basket, so let the redeemed sing 'til the trumpet sounds. If this is your home, we have work to do. The answer lies within us. The power lies within us. If we're not careful, our end times theology will keep us twiddling our thumbs, waiting on the rapture. The greatest hope for America is for the Church to rise up in radical love and supernatural power. To truly believe the Bible and begin walking out our faith with conviction unlike any other generation.

I'm believing God for a shift to come to my country. I'm believing for such an authentic repentance from the bad habits and poor mindset we've developed as a whole that it reforms the Church of America as we know it. As the Church is reformed, so will be the rest of the nation. Instead of entertainment driven songs, we'll worship the King out of sacrifice. Instead of a self-centered desire for churchgoers, a selfless life-giving passion will burst forth from true Christians. Instead of casual surface relationships, challenging and accountability-encouraged relationships where iron actually sharpens iron will rule the day. We'll trade in our comfortable atmospheres for the provoking, weighty presence of God. We'll let His Spirit direct our agendas not our clocks. We'll meet the needs of others, no matter the cost. We'll give until it hurts. We'll consider others better than ourselves. We'll see the potential through the eyes of the Spirit. We'll see the lost through the eyes of the Savior. We'll see the saved through the eyes of the Father. We'll see ourselves through the eyes of our God.

The Father is in the business of taking unlikely individuals and turning them into spiritual catalysts for revival. At one point in time, America was the choice option for such a move of God; in recent years, she's become the unlikely choice. That's only discouraging if you believe that He is not the same yesterday, today, and forever. The more unlikely it may seem for America to bend her knee to Almighty God perhaps the more likely it will happen. Obviously I'm not rooting for things to get worse so that they can get better. Take a look around, turn on the news, read the paper, scroll through social media; things are already bad enough. Amidst all the torment and tears, I can hear the Church praying again. Amidst all the bombing and gun shots, I can hear the Church singing again. Amidst all the fighting and hating, I can feel the Church loving again.

This verse always keeps me in the right perspective: **"If My people who are called by My name will humble themselves, and pray and seek My face, and turn from their wicked ways, then I will hear from heaven, and will forgive their sin and heal their land" (2 Chron. 7:14 NKJV).** It's a conditional promise and I don't want to forfeit the incredible blessing because I couldn't follow through on my end of the bargain. I want to humble myself, pray, and seek His face and turn from my wicked ways. Only then will He hear from Heaven, forgive our sins and restore/heal our land. What we do individually has repercussions nationally. This is bigger than us. How many are counting on you or me to take this seriously? How much of the nation will be affected if I never step into my destiny? The United States of America and far beyond her borders are crying out for you and me to walk like Christ walked the earth even if those people don't realize that's what they're asking for. They need Jesus, but they don't know that Jesus is His name. The Church, in her potential, is the much-needed answer for the country we love and it all resides within the everyday believer determining to be more than they currently are. To be all He's paid for them to be. To burn with a contagious fire that they are unashamed to fuel and spread as long as they live.

A prayer from President George Washington's prayer journal reads, "*Oh, eternal and everlasting God, direct my thoughts, words and work. Wash away my sins in the immaculate blood of the Lamb and purge my heart by Thy Holy Spirit. Daily, frame me more and more in the*

likeness of Thy son, Jesus Christ, that living in Thy fear, and dying in Thy favor, I may in thy appointed time obtain the resurrection of the justified unto eternal life. Bless, O Lord, the whole race of mankind and let the world be filled with the knowledge of Thee and Thy son, Jesus Christ."
"Blessed *is* the nation whose God *is* the LORD,
The people He has chosen as His own inheritance" (Psa.
33:12 NKJV).

For more information, including booking, events, ministry updates and detailed information on the author Josiah Elias please visit: www.josiahelias.com
or simply email: Elias.Josiah@gmail.com

Josiah is currently on staff at Faith Chapel in
San Diego, CA
as the Young Adults Pastor.
Faith Chapel
9400 Campo Rd
Spring Valley, CA 91977
www.faithchapelsd.com
@faithchapelsd
One Accord Young Adults Ministry
@oneaccordsd
#oneaccordfamily